MW01152622

Jesus' family and friends include:

_____

_____

_____

_____

_____

We began reading this book on

Date: _____

LOYOLA KIDS BOOK of
JESUS, HIS FAMILY, AND HIS FRIENDS

LOYOLA PRESS.
A JESUIT MINISTRY

www.loyolapress.com

Copyright © 2024 Loretta Pehanich, text
All rights reserved.

Scripture texts in this work are taken from the *New American Bible*, revised edition
© 2010, 1991, 1986, 1970 by Confraternity of Christian Doctrine, Washington, D.C.,
and are used by permission of the copyright owner. All Rights Reserved. No part of the
New American Bible may be reproduced in any form without permission in writing from
the copyright owner.

Cover art credits: invincible_bulldog/iStock/Getty Images
Interior art credits: TopVectors/iStock/Getty Images, SH-Vector/Shutterstock,
invincible_bulldog/iStock/Getty Images, Mikhail Seleznev/iStock/Getty Images,
undrey/iStock/Getty Images, Kudryavtsev Pavel/iStock/Getty Images, Loyola Press

ISBN: 978-0-8294-5489-5
Library of Congress Control Number: 2023952616

Printed in China
24 25 26 27 28 29 30 31 32 33 DC 10 9 8 7 6 5 4 3 2 1

LOYOLA KIDS BOOK *of*

JESUS, HIS FAMILY, AND HIS FRIENDS

LORETTA PEHANICH

LOYOLAPRESS.
A JESUIT MINISTRY
Chicago

CONTENTS

Part 2: Jesus and His Friends

Part 3: Jesus and Friendship

Part 4: Jesus Lives!

FOR ADULTS: HOW TO USE THIS BOOK

There's a kid in all of us. This book is for you, too. You may worry about how to teach children the faith. However, when Jesus said, "Let the little children come to me," he was basically saying, 'Leave it to me!' So relax and have fun!

Precious, powerful, and wonderful dialogue occurs when we set aside quality time to read aloud together. Adults are often surprised when they ask what children heard. You may be struck by Jesus calling a pair of brothers to him, while a child may be wondering about fishing. So start by asking what your young listener heard after sharing a story. Don't be afraid of silence. Give kids plenty of time to think. You can even pray for them while you wait for them to say something. Don't jump in too quickly!

Each person may wish to share what they found most interesting in a story. This is a great way to start. When you ask, "What did you hear?" children may shrug their shoulders. That's why conversation starters appear after each story. Your conversations may inspire additional chats with family members. Learn to be comfortable sitting quietly together. Pay attention to how God whispers thoughts, ideas, and insights into our heads. God surprises us when we make room for quiet.

Adults might want to make time to look over a chapter before reading it with a child and ponder the questions prayerfully. If you are puzzled by something, use the "Where to Find Out More" resources in each section.

Don't hesitate to use your imagination, and encourage children to do so too. Employing all five senses, think about what people might be saying or doing. Listen to the voices of Scripture. Let the story come alive. Be part of the story. Using this prayer method, kids can develop a contemplative awareness; they can hear God within.

Listening for God can feel intimidating, and children might digress into tangents about cows, donkeys, and animal rights. To get back on track, you might say, "Yes, that's important, but let's get back to how Jesus (is a friend, brother, etc.)."

We all need someone to talk to, even more so when it comes to spiritual topics. Some adults visit with spiritual directors to shed light on thoughts, ideas, and feelings that lead toward or away from God. A witness/companion can draw out deeper truths and foster growth.

You can be this listener for children by remaining aware that Jesus truly is present when you read and talk with them. *Let Jesus do the work.* Be at ease. It's not necessary for you to have all the answers. Humility in admitting we don't know everything is one way we imitate Jesus, and we can teach children this virtue also. (See Philippians 2:6–11.)

Every question can be brought to prayer. There is no one right way to pray. Children more easily learn to pray using their own words when they have a role model. Adults initially may feel self-conscious, but praying in your own words builds stronger relationships. Children learn, as St. Ignatius taught, that it is okay to speak casually when we pray, as if speaking to a friend. As we practice and learn to pray with children, we develop our own prayer as well.

Most of all, make reading this book a time for fun and wonder. Tell your own stories as they relate to those you are reading together. Laugh. Giggle. Be puzzled. All your emotions are raw material for God's visits with you. Prayer is a personal conversation with the God who loves us infinitely. Expect good things and ask God for the graces to enjoy learning together about Jesus, his family, and his friends.

HEY KIDS! AN INTRODUCTION

Jesus' life was full of people who loved and supported him. Some joined him on adventures, and some found him mysterious. This book will explore some of the amazing stories about Jesus that show us what family and friends meant to him and how he related to the people in his life.

Because he rose from the dead, Jesus still lives. Therefore, stories about him aren't finished. We experience new adventures with Jesus every day as we grow in our love for him and for the whole world.

One way to get to know Jesus better is to use prayerful imagination, which is a wonderful gift from God.

Think for a moment about the most delicious meal you can remember. The table might have a fancy tablecloth on it, and china dishes, and enough settings for the whole family to have dinner at Grandma's. Or maybe it's a birthday party with balloons, hot dogs, cake, ice cream, and friends your age. To you, the most delicious meal might be macaroni and cheese with just one other person. Guess what? You just used your imagination. What you imagined were real things.

Imagination is a wonderful ability, just like eyesight and hearing. God uses imagination to help us consider things in a new way.

As you read these stories, you are invited to imagine being present with Jesus—the most amazing and important person ever born—and to make friends with his friends and family.

Putting yourself in a Gospel story is a type of prayer encouraged by Ignatius of Loyola, who 500 years ago wrote a book, *The Spiritual Exercises*, that is still popular today.

God uses imaginations to plant inside us thoughts, ideas, and feelings that lead us to recognize his presence in our lives.

As we bring our thoughts and questions to Jesus, our conversations will connect our real life with Jesus' real life. We do this through prayer.

Good Question!

What is Prayer?

Prayer is simply a two-way conversation with God that includes time to speak, time to listen, and time for silence. It can happen anywhere, anytime.

Your feelings and thoughts could be a lot like the feelings and thoughts Jesus had at your age. You can talk to Jesus about this aloud or silently. God hears your thoughts. You can also listen for an idea that God might put into your mind, or a feeling he might place in your heart. Listening in silence is a way to pray.

Jesus led an adventurous life on earth, and you might be surprised by the powerful stories about him and the many people—family and friends—he cared about.

The more we discover about who Jesus was, and who he is in our lives now, the closer we will become as friends. Jesus is eager to be in relationship with every human being. And the way to grow a friendship is to get to know each other. That's what this book is about.

Blessed are the peacemakers,

for they will be called children of God.

—*Matthew 5:9*

PART 1:
JESUS AND HIS FAMILY

He is the image of the invisible God,

the firstborn of all creation.

—*Colossians 1:15*

Who Was Jesus?
Who IS Jesus?

You might wonder what Jesus was like as a child. Did he have pets? Did he do chores, or sometimes forget to do them? Did he make mistakes? Did he study and pray all the time?

And what was it like as he grew up? Did relatives live with Jesus and his parents? Did he call someone uncle who wasn't related but who was a close family friend? Were there kids in his neighborhood who became lifelong friends?

Jesus was the son of Mary, and it's possible he looked like her. He is also the son of God, and the Bible tells us that Jesus is the image of God, his heavenly Father. God sent Jesus to show us how to live and how we could be in heaven with God forever.

Jesus learned many things from family members, and he enjoyed traditions from his ancestors, just as you do. His extended family included some interesting people. Read on to learn about Jesus' relatives and to explore some of his family's stories. They are your stories, too.

Jesus lived at a time quite different from ours. His world had no cameras, television, internet, electric plugs, lights, cell phones, or all kinds of things invented later. Therefore, we don't know everything about his life.

Jesus was human. He was a person just like us in every way, except he never sinned. At the same time, Jesus is also God, the second person in the Holy Trinity. God wanted to live among his people 2,000 years ago, to live in simplicity, and to love. He did these things in the person of his son, Jesus.

Good Question!

What is the Trinity?

There is only one God. God is the Father, the Son Jesus, and Holy Spirit all in one. This belief in the Holy Trinity is a central mystery of our faith.

Other than a few passages in the Gospels, no written records tell us what Jesus did for his first thirty years. But historians wrote about the government back then, and we know the geography of his country. We can assume that in those thirty "hidden" years he lived an ordinary life, just as we do. We can be sure he had his share of fun as well as his share of sadness. We know that loving God and loving people was—and still is—the most important thing to Jesus.

Compared to grown-ups, little children take smaller steps, eat smaller bites of food, and learn smaller pieces of information. God knew that revealing himself in all his glory would be too much for his children. God knew, however, that we could relate to another human being without getting scared and running away. So, God chose to become human to show people a perfect example of how to love. In fact, Jesus came into this world as a helpless little baby and grew up like the rest of us. Yet, he came to show us what God is like. You can think of Jesus as God's selfie!

Good Question!

What does God look like?

Jesus came to earth to show us the face of the invisible God. God "looks like" Jesus.

Jesus said that whoever has seen Jesus has seen God the Father. Plus, you look like God because you also were created in God's image. Many things about you are just like God. It could be the joy you bring to others, or how easily you show love, or how you cry with someone who's hurting.

When you look at another person, and you see love or mercy, you are recognizing the image of God.

God came to save us so we could be in heaven with him forever. God so loved humanity that God became one of us. The word that refers to God becoming human is Incarnation.

The more you know about Jesus, the easier it will be to see the way Jesus sees. This surely will lead you to joy.

CONVERSATION STARTERS

The Bible is full of great stories. When might be a good time to add Bible reading to your day?

In what ways do you reflect the image of God?

WHERE TO FIND OUT MORE

God Didn't Send Jesus into the World to Condemn People:
John 3:17

◇◇◇◇◇◇◇◇◇◇◇◇◇◇◇◇◇◇◇◇◇

A PRAYER

Our Father, you created so many wonderful things,
like families and friendship. Thank you for sending your son into this world.
I am glad you want us to be friends. Amen.

◇◇◇◇◇◇◇◇◇◇◇◇◇◇◇◇◇◇◇◇◇

Jesus' Family Tree

Families connect people in various ways. One way to show family relationships is to draw branches on a tree. The trunk might be your grandparents. Your mom and her siblings would be represented by branches reaching out from the trunk. Your dad would be shown on the tree, too, with you and any siblings you may have growing outward from your parents. Cousins would be branching up from aunts and uncles, and so on. Some family trees are complex and full. Others don't have many people, but they represent families just the same.

Jesus' family tree is complicated, and the Bible is full of stories about his ancestors. Some of these stories are told in poems, and others include pages and pages of details.

Family trees are a way of showing how connected people are, even though not everyone lives together, or even at the same time. Just as branches depend on the tree's roots and trunk, family members need each other and rely on the strength of past generations in heaven to continue to pray for those of us still on earth.

People call Jesus' family history the Jesse Tree, after Jesse, who was King David's father.

King David ruled a thousand years before Jesus' birth. Before becoming king, David defended his people by defeating a fierce, giant warrior. When every trained soldier refused to go up against Goliath out of fear, David volunteered to go one-on-one with the bragging man who was much stronger than everyone. Even though David was still considered a boy, he stepped forward and knocked down the older and more experienced soldier, using only a slingshot. After Goliath died, the rest of Goliath's countrymen ran away. David's bravery became legendary.

David is credited with writing beautiful songs called psalms. Jesus prayed these psalms, and we pray them, too, every time we celebrate Mass or read them in the Bible. One of Jesus' titles, *Son of David*, refers to Jesus being king over everything.

Good Question!

What are psalms?

Psalms are song-like prayers that are packed with feelings and thoughts everyone experiences. The people of Israel collected psalms over hundreds of years. There are 150 psalms in the Book of Psalms in the Bible.

Just like any family, the Jesse Tree includes people who led virtuous lives, and others who made bad choices. God loved them all, and he also loves all of us no matter what. The stories of Jesus' long-ago relatives, including King David, are found in what Christians call the Old Testament. For example, an entire book in the Bible is devoted to stories about King David's great-grandmother, Ruth, who came from a foreign country called Moab. She married Boaz, who lived in Bethlehem, where Jesus was born many years later.

Good Question!

What is the Old Testament?

The Bible has two parts: The Old Testament tells stories of what happened before Jesus' birth. Another term for the Old Testament is the Hebrew Scriptures. The other part of the Bible, the New Testament, includes books written after Jesus was born.

Matthew's Gospel lists the generations in Jesus' family all the way back to Abraham, whom Christians (as well as Muslims and Jews) call *our father in faith*. We are branches of Abraham's family.

Abraham's son was Isaac, whose son Jacob wrestled with an angel and received a new name by which he was known from then on: Israel.

Israel made the mistake of favoring one of his sons, Joseph. This made his eleven *other* sons so jealous that they did a horrible thing: They sold Joseph into slavery in Egypt. However, God used their terrible choice to rescue all of Israel's family from a deadly famine. The food shortage caused Joseph's siblings and their families to move to Egypt, where they were welcomed by their brother Joseph, who was now a powerful leader. Eventually, these siblings became known as the twelve tribes of Israel. (Imagine all the relatives *they* had!)

Over time, Egyptians forgot the good deeds that Joseph did, and they enslaved the Israelites. Jesus' ancestors suffered much as enslaved persons, but they kept praying and begging God to help them. And of course, God did. The Israelites were led out of Egypt and returned to the land that had belonged to Abraham long before.

Good Question!

Who are the Israelites?

Jesus was born into a large extended family called the Israelites. The name originated with Jacob, who earned it by battling an angel. The word Israel means "Wrestles with God."

The Israelites had lots of adventures after leaving Egypt. Much later, and long after David was king, the twelve tribes split into a North Kingdom and a South Kingdom. The Northern Kingdom was defeated by the Assyrians and the people were scattered throughout the region of Samaria. Later, the Southern Kingdom was defeated by the Babylonians and their leaders were taken into exile. They cried and wrote about their troubles in Babylon. Meanwhile, the people who didn't get captured and taken out of their country started to forget their traditions, eventually copying the practices of their enemies who had moved in. This included honoring false gods. When the Jews who had been in Babylon returned and rebuilt the temple, a sharp division arose between them and those who had blended into Samaritan culture.

More generations passed. By the time Jesus was born, the Israelites were suffering under a foreign power, the Roman Empire.

Jesus' complex family tree is a lot like many of our complicated families today. It includes too many stories to mention here. Jesus' family was far from perfect. God chose that Jesus would be born into a simple family, in humble circumstances, in a town so small that people didn't consider it important at all. But God had a plan and good reasons for choosing this family for Jesus.

CONVERSATION STARTERS

Why do you think God wanted Jesus to live an ordinary life in a simple village?

What do you know about your ancestors? What religious traditions did they practice? What does your family look like today? What people are included in it?

WHERE TO FIND OUT MORE

Sprouting from Jesse: Isaiah 11:1

Jesus' Ancestors: Luke 3:23–38

Genealogy: Matthew 1:1–17

Other Ancestors: Ruth 1:1–4:22

A PRAYER

Loving God, you gave me a family that includes
people I don't even know, people who already died,
and people who are yet to be born. Thank you for everyone in my family.
Someday we hope to meet in heaven, and it will be wonderful.
Thank you for watching over my family until then. Amen.

Many are the women of proven worth,

but you have excelled them all.

—*Proverbs 31:29*

Jesus' Mother

No one ever born was quite like Mary.

When the angel Gabriel appeared to her saying, "Hail, Mary!" and told her that God wanted her to become the mother of Jesus, even though she wasn't even married yet, Mary said yes to God. The brave girl was certainly shocked when a supernatural being suddenly appeared in her house, but she humbly listened, and pondered. She could not know what her life would be like, but that didn't matter. God wanted something from her, and she told the angel that she was God's servant. Whatever God wanted, she would do.

Soon her life was filled with adventures, difficulties, and even sorrows. But she never stopped loving God or doing everything possible to support her son. Now in heaven, Mary remains our ally: she's a great listener, she *always* wants what's best for us, and she always points us to her son, Jesus.

Mary was generous and eager to serve others. For example, rather than focus on herself while she was pregnant, Mary traveled a great distance to help her cousin Elizabeth who was about to have a baby six months before Mary's son would be born.

Mary burst into praise for God and what God was accomplishing when Elizabeth said, "Blessed are you among women!" Mary was like that: Always ready to ponder God's greatness, mercy, and power. She delighted in saying good things about God, who humbles proud people and feeds hungry people while sending the rich away empty. She also said that God remembers every promise of love in every generation.

Gentle and full of God's gifts (called graces), Mary kept Jesus safe, taught him right from wrong, and nurtured him. A woman full of goodness and devotion, she did the kinds of things moms do today to care for their children. She was a helpful friend to others and a loving wife to Joseph. And she was more.

Good Question!

What makes Jesus' mother different?

Jesus' mom was born without any sin. The church gave Mary the title Immaculate Conception to recognize this, and celebrates it with a feast every year on December 8. We celebrate Mary's birthday on September 8.

Mary participated actively in Jesus' ministry. For example, she encouraged him to do his first miracle at a wedding in Cana. And she stood by him as he was suffering a painful death on the cross. Right before he died, Jesus asked his close friend John to care for his mother, and from that day on, John watched over Mary as if she were his own mother.

Jesus' request to John, *"Behold, your mother"* (John 19:27) is one of the reasons Catholics consider Mary to be our spiritual mother. She provided a great example of courage and fidelity. We can imitate her during our own difficult times.

Good Question!

What is fidelity?

Fidelity is the act of remaining faithful (loyal and committed). Even when times are tough, a person of fidelity remains true and supportive.

After Jesus returned to heaven, which is an event known as the Ascension, Mary stayed in touch with his friends and Apostles. She wanted to encourage and support their efforts at building up the Body of Christ, a term we use sometimes to refer to the Church. Why? Every person who loves Jesus is a part of the "Body of Christ." Just as our bodies have many parts and each has a job to do, the Church needs all of us, with Jesus as our "head," to work together. And Mary is essential to this body. You could even say she mothered the Church into being.

People today refer to Mary using many different names of love, respect, and affection. These titles help us show gratitude for her prayers *for* us and *with* us. Some of these names are Our Blessed Mother, Help of the Sick, Refuge of Sinners, Cause of Our Joy, Untier of Knots, Our Lady of Tenderness, Our Lady of Providence, Our Lady of Confidence, Our Lady of Guidance, and Our Lady of Hope.

Mary is also called *Our Lady of* cities wherever apparitions, or spiritual visions, of her occurred. These apparitions are memorialized in names such as Our Lady of Fátima, Our Lady of Guadalupe, and Our Lady of Lourdes.

We look to Mary as our mother, and she is the Mother of God. Jesus' Mother Mary is our mother, too.

One girl who understood this well was Catherine Labouré, who was born in France in 1806. She had ten brothers and sisters, and was only nine years old when her mother died. Catherine went to the statue of Mary that was in her home, and she used her imagination to feel Mary's presence right there beside her. Through her tears, Catherine said, "Now, dear Blessed Mother, you will be my mother." She drew strength from knowing that God's own mother would intercede for her.

Good Question!

What does it mean to intercede?

It means asking for someone's help. For example, maybe you need help from your mom or dad in talking to your teacher about a problem you're having in school. When this happens, your parent would be interceding on your behalf. In the same way, when we pray to Mary or other saints, we are asking them to intercede with their own prayers to God, to whom *all* power belongs.

At age 23, Catherine joined the Daughters of Charity, religious sisters who live together in homes called convents and who devote their lives to serving God by caring for people who are sick or elderly. One night in 1830, an angel woke Catherine and led her to the chapel. There, Catherine saw Mary sitting in a chair near the altar. Catherine knelt at Mary's feet and placed her hands in Mary's lap. Mary visited Catherine two more times that year. Mary asked Catherine to create a special medal that people could wear and use when they prayed. When the medal was made, many who wore it experienced miracles, which is why it became known as the Miraculous Medal.

This is only one of countless true stories about Mary, the remarkable things she has done as our mother, and the miracles that have happened thanks to her intercession.

CONVERSATION STARTERS

What does it mean to consider Mary as your mother?

Knowing that Mary helped build up the Church, the Body of Christ, how might you help the Church, which is God's family?

Which of the titles of Mary listed above do you like best? Which are difficult to understand?

WHERE TO FIND OUT MORE

Jesus Gives Us Mary as Mother: John 19:25–27

◇◇◇◇◇◇◇◇◇◇◇◇◇◇◇◇◇◇◇◇◇◇◇

A PRAYER

Hail, Mary, full of grace,
the Lord is with thee.
Blessed art thou among women
and blessed is the fruit of thy womb, Jesus.
Holy Mary, Mother of God,
pray for us sinners,
now and at the hour of our death. Amen.

◇◇◇◇◇◇◇◇◇◇◇◇◇◇◇◇◇◇◇◇◇◇◇

Jesus' Earthly Father

Families come in many sizes. Some have a mom and dad and their children. Some are one parent and a child. Some include a dozen children, with stepsiblings and stepparents, or foster brothers and foster sisters, extra sets of grandparents, and people who are not related at all, but who are important participants in family life.

Jesus had two fathers: Joseph, his earthly father, who was a builder or carpenter and craftsman, and God.

Joseph was an honorable man. Like Joseph in the Old Testament (and many other people), Jesus' foster father heard God communicate with him in dreams. And Joseph obeyed when he understood what God wanted him to do, like the time God told Joseph to marry Mary because the father of her baby was God. Joseph did accept Mary as his wife.

Joseph worked with wood. Think about people you see on construction sites. It takes a great deal of skill to build things. Joseph probably taught Jesus all about his craft.

The Bible doesn't say much about Joseph, and therefore some people think of him as a quiet yet strong father. God the Father had to be close to Joseph because raising Jesus was a serious responsibility, and Joseph must have known how to pray to God the Father for help.

We do have stories of Joseph protecting Jesus and Mary from harm. For example, Joseph heard God say in a dream that his child Jesus was in danger from the jealous King Herod. Joseph woke up and realized he had to get Jesus to safety. He bundled up the little family and fled. Joseph heard from God again after moving the family to Egypt, where they lived as refugees for some time. Joseph dreamed that it was safe to return to the land of Israel. So he started to pack up the family for another move. But then he had *another* dream, so instead of settling where they lived before, Joseph realized that the holy family would be safer in Galilee.

Good Question!

What is a refugee?

Refugees are people who leave their home country because it is no longer safe for them to live there. They are forced out by war, natural disasters, and other tragic circumstances.

We don't know exactly when Joseph died, but we do know that his wife, Mary, stood at the foot of Jesus' cross without her husband. If Joseph had been alive, Jesus would not have asked his beloved friend John to take care of his mother.

Sometimes children are named after their grandparents or someone else in the family. Joseph did not get to name his foster son. God the Father picked out the name for his baby: Jesus. The Angel Gabriel told Mary to use that name.

Did you ever wonder if Jesus knew his grandparents? Mary's parents were named Anna and Joachim. They prayed for a child for a long time. It is possible that they lived near Joseph and Mary and played with Jesus as he grew up.

Many people wish we knew more about Joseph and the ordinary childhood that Jesus lived, because Jesus was the most important person ever born. But we can imagine Jesus growing up and learning how to do things and how to get along with others, just as we must do.

Jesus said we can call God our Father. In this sense, Jesus can be viewed as our sibling. Loving actions also create family relationships. As Jesus put it, *"My mother and my brothers are those who hear the word of God and act on it"* (Luke 8:21).

Everyone who is baptized is adopted into God's family. At baptism, the presider who guides the celebration will say, "The Christian community welcomes you with great joy. In its name I claim you for Christ our Savior by the sign of his cross." You are claimed. You belong.

Joseph had the great responsibility and privilege of taking care of Jesus as he grew, including teaching him how to pray to God the Father. He must have done a good job at this, because we know that Jesus turned to God, his "Abba," affectionately, obediently, and trustingly.

CONVERSATION STARTERS

Name some important qualities and characteristics of fathers.

If you could talk to Joseph, what would you want to know?

WHERE TO FIND OUT MORE

God Names Jesus: Luke 1:30–38

Four Dreams:

> **Joseph, Don't Fear Marrying Mary:** Matthew 1:18–25

> **Joseph, Leave Bethlehem:** Matthew 2:13–15

> **It's Safe to Go Back to Israel:** Matthew 2:19–21

> **Don't Move to Judea:** Matthew 2:22–23

A Different Joseph Dreamed, Too: Genesis 37:5–11 and
40:4—41:42

◇◇◇◇◇◇◇◇◇◇◇◇◇◇◇◇◇◇◇

A PRAYER

Holy God,
you knew you would name your child Jesus before time began.
I praise you, God! You are incredible.
I love you. Amen.

◇◇◇◇◇◇◇◇◇◇◇◇◇◇◇◇◇◇◇

Jesus' Birthplace

Jesus wasn't born in a hospital, or even in a house. He would have been born at home except for a census, which is a method of counting the number of people living in any given place. The Romans wanted to know how many people lived under their control so that they could charge them taxes. To do this, the descendants of the twelve tribes had to journey to the places where their ancestors were born. Joseph's father, and grandfather, and great-grandfather could trace their family all the way back to the famous King David. This was called being "of the house of David." King David was born about a thousand years before Jesus.

According to Luke's Gospel, Joseph and his family would have to go to "the city of David," which was Bethlehem. Both Mary and Joseph could trace their family roots back to King David. That's why Mary and Joseph were traveling when it came time for Jesus to be born.

Jostling up and down on a donkey for miles and miles could have made Mary feel sick. Dust probably stung her throat as others in their traveling group shuffled along. The roads were rough, not paved. Perhaps Mary also walked beneath the blazing sun part of the way.

Good Question!

Can I visit where Jesus was born?

Yes, you can visit Bethlehem. Modern life has transformed the streets, and new buildings and churches have been built. Many people make prayer-centered trips called pilgrimages to Bethlehem. Maybe someday you will, too.

When Mary and Joseph arrived in Bethlehem, people coming for the census crowded into the town. Finding anywhere to stay was difficult, especially if you didn't have much money. Mary and Joseph were not wealthy. Joseph knocked at many doors, but all he could find for their lodging was a stable. Imagine Mary surrounded by animals while giving birth to her child!

God sent Jesus into the world just like everyone else: an infant born from a woman. God could have chosen for Jesus to appear on earth suddenly, as an adult. But God wanted Jesus to go through everything people do, including birth as a baby. Jesus relied on Mary's body and blood for his growth. Mary may have struggled to stay healthy. She needed rest so that her body could birth God as a human. What an amazing mystery that God chose for Jesus to be utterly dependent on his parents! Jesus experienced being an infant who needed his parents for food, clothing, shelter, and protection.

CONVERSATION STARTERS

Why do you think God chose for Jesus to be born to a family that was not wealthy or powerful?

What part of the story about Jesus' birth most captures your imagination?

WHERE TO FIND OUT MORE

Jesus' Family Tree: Matthew 1:1–17 and Luke 3:23–38

Jesus' Birth, Kings' Visit: Matthew 1:18—2:23

Jesus' Birth, Shepherds' Visit: Luke 2:1–21

He Became Poor to Make Us Rich: 2 Corinthians 8:9

A PRAYER

Take a few quiet moments.
Imagine traveling with Mary and Joseph to Bethlehem.
Trees dot the landscape. Maybe you offer Mary some water
when the group stops to rest. Do you feel excited that Jesus is about to be born?
Offer help to the couple because they are far from home.
After some silent moments, ask God any question you like,
and finish with Amen.

[There is] one God and Father of all,

who is over all and through all and in all.

—Ephesians 4:6

Jesus' Other Family Members

In Jesus' extended family was a man named Zechariah who served in the temple, and people thought very highly of him. Zechariah and his wife, Elizabeth, who was Mary's cousin, had no children. They were so old that it seemed they would never have any.

One day, Zechariah entered the holiest room in the temple. This was a privilege reserved for priests. He never expected to see an angel there. The angel was a messenger from God, sent to give Zechariah good news.

Other people in history had visits from angels, including Abraham, Israel (also known as Jacob), shepherds when Jesus was born, Peter the Apostle, the women at Jesus' tomb on the day he rose from the dead, and many others. Because people were surprised to see an angel, usually the angel would say, "Do not be afraid."

The angel that appeared to Zechariah was Gabriel, the same angel who had visited Mary to ask her to be the mother of Jesus. Gabriel told Zechariah that Elizabeth would have a baby who should be named John. Gabriel also said that John would become as great as the famous prophet Elijah, who lived about 700 years before Jesus was born. Elijah's unshakable faith in God led him to perform miracles, and he tried to convince the Israelites to turn away from worshiping false Gods.

Can you imagine what Zechariah thought? He knew that a prophet is someone who speaks wisely about what will happen in the future, and teaches. How could his own yet-to-be born son be such a person?

Zechariah was dedicated to God, but that didn't mean he never had moments of doubt. The angel's predictions sounded ridiculous to Zechariah. He chose not to believe the angel. The consequence was that Zechariah lost his ability to speak.

As we learned in the section on Jesus' mother, when Mary was pregnant with Jesus, she visited her cousin Elizabeth and Zechariah. The moment that the two women came face to face, Elizabeth felt her unborn child move inside her, and Elizabeth immediately understood this as a sign that Mary's baby was special. By giving his mother this signal about Jesus, the baby inside Elizabeth began his life as a prophet even before his birth.

When the baby was born, everyone expected that he would be named after his dad, which was the custom back then. However, his mother Elizabeth announced that he would be named John. When they turned to Zechariah for his reaction, he signaled for a tablet, and wrote, *"John is his name"* (Luke 1:63). The moment he wrote those words, his voice returned, and he immediately began praising God. People were stunned at the miraculous recovery of Zechariah's voice. It was another clear sign that John too would be someone very special.

The Bible doesn't say whether John and Jesus visited one another, or whether their families socialized. But it is possible that they did things together just as you and your family do with relatives, friends, and other families.

The next time John is mentioned in the Bible, he is an adult. Known as "John the Baptist," he baptized people in the Jordan River after asking them to turn away from sin. When they agreed to repent, he plunged them into the Jordan River as a symbol that they had been washed clean of sin.

Good Questions!

What is sin? What does it mean to repent?

Sin refers to thoughts, words, or actions that cause damage to our relationship with God and others. Sin might also be something good that we fail to do. Because God loves every person, when we harm others, we work against what God wants for us and for them. To repent means saying you are sorry, and doing something to make up for the harm you have caused. Repentance (penance) is often accompanied by offering prayers or sacrificing something.

One day, Jesus, who was only six months younger than his cousin John, came to the river to be baptized. At first, John hesitated. He did not understand why Jesus would want to be baptized by him. John knew that Jesus was different; he had never sinned and so he didn't need to repent. But Jesus insisted. When Jesus came up out of the water, God said, *"This is my beloved Son, with whom I am well pleased"* (Matthew 3:17).

When Jesus left John, he went to the desert to pray alone. John continued baptizing more and more people. He pointed to Jesus as the one sent from God to save the whole world.

CONVERSATION STARTERS

Who named you, and why did they choose that name? If you don't know, you can ask.

Who are some other people you know with the same name?

Why is a person's name important?

WHERE TO FIND OUT MORE

Speechless Dad: Luke 1:5–22, 57–66

Zechariah's Canticle ('canticle' is another word for song, or hymn)**:** Luke 1:67–79

◇◇◇◇◇◇◇◇◇◇◇◇◇◇◇◇◇◇◇◇◇

A PRAYER

Let's use words similar to those Zechariah used when his voice returned:

Blessed be God who has come to us and set us free!
In the tender compassion of our God, goodness shall shine
on those who dwell in darkness, and God will guide us to peace.
Thank you, God, for loving us so much. Amen.

◇◇◇◇◇◇◇◇◇◇◇◇◇◇◇◇◇◇◇◇◇

Growing Up

Jesus grew up in a loving home, supported by humble parents. Jesus had lots of experiences, most likely played like other kids do, and obeyed his parents. But the day-to-day details of what happened in Jesus' childhood and teenage years remain a mystery to us. We wish we knew more about him during those early years.

One story we do have occurred when Jesus was twelve years old.

Mary, Joseph, and Jesus took a family trip every year to Jerusalem. They traveled in a group with friends and members of their community to celebrate Passover. The people in the caravan may have been neighbors, work friends, friends who were like family, and people in other villages who joined the group along the way.

Good Question!

What is Passover?

Passover is a Jewish holiday celebrated ever since Moses led the descendants of Israel out of Egypt. Families gather to remember that God saved them from slavery. The Passover meal includes unleavened bread, wine, bitter herbs, lamb, and ritual prayers and songs.

This particular year, after celebrating Passover, Mary and Joseph's family and friends gathered to make the trip home. In those days, the men often traveled in one group while the women traveled in another, so it's easy to see how Mary and Joseph might have thought that Jesus was with the other parent or with friends or cousins.

Mary and Joseph traveled for a full day before they realized Jesus was missing. That meant they had to travel a full day *back* to the big city.

We don't know the reason Jesus didn't leave with the caravan. Maybe he thought he could go off by himself because, in Jewish tradition, someone who is twelve is considered old enough to start making responsible decisions. Or maybe Jesus was daydreaming and didn't realize everyone was leaving. Whatever the reason, Jesus found himself apart from his family for three days.

What must that have felt like for him? Was he hungry? Where did he sleep? Were strangers kind to him? We can use our imaginations to think about his experience.

After three days, his anxious parents found Jesus in the temple, talking with teachers and other experts in the Jewish faith. Mary and Joseph must have breathed a huge sigh of relief. Their son was safe! As for the temple elders, they were astonished with Jesus' knowledge, and impressed by the questions he asked. Perhaps Jesus hadn't left with the caravan because he thought it was time for him to stay at the temple and learn more about his heavenly Father.

Surprised to see his parents so upset, Jesus asked why they had been looking all over the city. He was puzzled that they wouldn't have known where he could be found: at the house of God, his Father. Even though Jesus was intelligent, thoughtful, and obedient, maybe he was too young to understand that Mary and Joseph would be worried because they loved him so much and God had given them the responsibility to keep him safe.

Jesus began to see important truths about being part of a family after this adventure in Jerusalem, including the fact that parents often see a situation differently from the way their children do.

CONVERSATION STARTERS

Have you ever been lost for more than an hour? If so, what was that like for you?

What are some good choices to make if you get lost?

What can you do if you feel like God doesn't know where you are? What might you say to Jesus if you feel lost?

WHERE TO FIND OUT MORE

God, You Know Me: Psalm 139

Jesus Lost: Luke 2:41–52

A PRAYER

Gentle Jesus, growing up takes time.
Sometimes I wonder what the future holds.
Help me remember that, whatever happens, you are with me.
Even when I feel alone or lost, you know where I am.
Thank you. Amen.

Jesus and His Mom at a Wedding

As Jesus grew, his circle of friends and family did, too. Among the people he knew was a couple getting married in Cana, a town near Nazareth. Jesus loved visiting with people, and his mother was also invited to this wedding. Mary understood that Jesus, being both God and human, cared deeply about every person, and he considered every family as his very own. That's why she knew she could ask Jesus to help when something went wrong at the wedding banquet.

You may have heard of miracles. That's when something happens that seems impossible. Of course, nothing is impossible for God, who wants all people to realize we are one giant human family.

Jesus was about thirty years old when his mother asked him to do something out of the ordinary for the people celebrating the wedding.

Perhaps Jesus was dancing or talking with friends or happily watching the bride and groom and their guests. He didn't notice that anything was wrong, but his mother did. The guests had finished all the wine. In the days before refrigerators, everyone drank wine as a common beverage. Running out of drinks at a wedding would be a terrible embarrassment for the hosts. Mary noticed the shortage, and she told Jesus. Jesus did not answer his mother in a way that sounded like he intended to do anything about it. In fact, he didn't seem to think this problem was his business. But Mary knew her son very well. She simply walked over to the servers and instructed them to do whatever Jesus told them to do.

Sure enough, Jesus did not let her down. He told the servers to fill six empty stone jars with water.

Good Question!

How much wine did Jesus create from water?

These six jars were *enormous*. Each one held between twenty and thirty gallons. Imagine six different piles of plastic gallon milk jugs, with thirty jugs in each pile. If you stacked your milk jugs together, they would be about the size of a large van: six feet high and ten feet long! From those six jars of water, Jesus created between 120 and 180 gallons of wine.

The servers filled the six jars to the brim with water. But when it was poured out again, it had become wine. And Jesus had performed his first public miracle.

When the head waiter tasted it, he couldn't hide his amazement at how delicious it was. He asked why they hadn't served this spectacular wine first.

After that miracle, Jesus spent the next three years traveling and telling people about God, working more miracles, and demonstrating how to love others. In the future, Jesus would use wine at his Last Supper, when he offered it, along with bread, as his body and blood. To this day, every time we attend Mass and join in the heavenly banquet, we receive the body and blood of Jesus under the appearance of bread and wine.

CONVERSATION STARTERS

Why is it important for a family or community to have celebrations?

We can follow Mary's advice to do whatever Jesus tells us. What do you think Jesus is asking you to do?

Can you think of some reasons why Mary asked Jesus to perform his first miracle at this celebration?

WHERE TO FIND OUT MORE

Wedding at Cana: John 2:1–12

A PRAYER

*Take a few quiet moments to imagine Jesus
arriving at a celebration you are attending.
How does he participate and interact with others?
Talk to Jesus. Thank him for inviting you to his heavenly banquet.
Finish with Amen.*

As a mother comforts her child,

so I will comfort you [says the Lord].

—*Isaiah 66:13*

Jesus' Extraordinary Concern for Families

The stories that follow reveal more ways that Jesus demonstrated love and concern for families, as he did at the wedding feast in Cana. Jesus felt great compassion for families suffering in various ways. Jesus' feelings were obvious when he came upon people in need, whether it was a dad worried about his daughter, sisters crying about the death of their brother, or siblings having trouble forgiving one another. Jesus could do something to help.

And Jesus still does. Each of us is very important to Jesus, no matter how small we think our problems are. Jesus can give us courage when someone in our family is sick. Jesus can transform any situation, even if the transformation doesn't happen right away. Jesus is planning to eliminate all sicknesses and problems in the biggest family reunion ever: heaven. And *that* is really good news.

Good Question!

Does Jesus still cure people in families today?

Yes. Miracles happen all the time. Jesus works through doctors, nurses, moms, dads, and many other people. Medicine might not seem miraculous in the same way as Jesus' dramatic miracles but it sure can be. Likewise, Jesus can bring about spiritual and emotional healing. Jesus also works miracles today through saints and his mother. For example, ever since Mary appeared to a young girl named Bernadette in Lourdes, France, and healings started occurring, people visit that city to ask Mary to intercede on their behalf with Jesus, who is the source of all miraculous healings. Many miracles continue to happen.

A FATHER AND DAUGHTER

Jairus was a leader in the Jewish community, and he was desperate. His twelve-year-old daughter was dying. No treatments helped. What could he do? He'd heard about Jesus healing others. So Jairus decided to go looking for Jesus. When he found him, the distraught father fell at Jesus' feet and asked for help. Jesus understood the love this man had for his daughter. After all, Jesus loved his mother and father deeply. The great importance of family was something Jesus and Jairus had in common.

Jesus agreed to go to Jairus's house. However, on his way there, some people told Jairus not to bother bringing Jesus to his house because Jairus's daughter had died already. Jesus told Jairus, *"Do not be afraid; just have faith"* (Mark 5:36).

Jairus made a choice to believe that Jesus could bring his dead daughter back to life, and they kept walking. When they got to Jairus's house, people outside were creating quite a commotion, wailing and crying. It must have tested Jairus's faith, but he kept on believing that Jesus could help. The first thing Jesus did when he went into the house was to shoo everyone outside. He allowed only the girl's parents and his three close friends (the brothers James and John, and Peter) to stay inside.

The girl's mother and father led Jesus to where the dead girl lay.

Jesus took her by the hand and said, *"Little girl, I say to you, arise!"* (Mark 5:41).

And she did!

Jesus demonstrated compassion for this family by bringing the child back to life.

CONVERSATION STARTERS

Imagine that you are Jairus's daughter. What would you say to Jesus when he took you by the hand and restored you to life?

When have you prayed for someone who was sick? How did it feel to ask for Jesus' help?

How have you been cared for when you were sick?

WHERE TO FIND OUT MORE

Jairus and His Daughter: Luke 8:49–56 and Mark 5:21–24, 35–43

Fear Is Useless: Mark 5:36

◇◇◇◇◇◇◇◇◇◇◇◇◇◇◇◇◇◇◇◇◇

A PRAYER

Jesus, you healed so many people. People unable to walk could suddenly dance; a man with a withered hand was suddenly complete; and other suffering people were cured wherever you went. Help me to be compassionate like you. Give me the grace to care for others who are sick, sad, or in need. Thanks! Amen.

◇◇◇◇◇◇◇◇◇◇◇◇◇◇◇◇◇◇◇◇◇

A MOTHER TOO SICK TO SERVE

One day, when Jesus went over to his friend Simon's house, members of the family asked Jesus to help the mother. Her skin was burning hot, but she was shivering. A high fever can be deadly, and the family had no medicine to reduce the fever. When Jesus saw the woman, he told the fever to leave. And it did. She immediately got better. The family was able to continue on as before.

To thank him, the mother happily prepared food and refreshments for Jesus and his friends. By the time the sun went down that day, people throughout the area had heard about the healing. They brought many sick people to Simon's house. Jesus laid his hands on each person and cured them all.

Early the next morning, Jesus left Simon's home and went off to a quiet place to pray. Jesus always made time for listening to and speaking with his Father. Crowds went looking for Jesus because of the healings he had performed the previous night. When they found Jesus, they begged him to stay in their town. Kindly, he said no, explaining that he needed to travel to other places and tell other people about God's love and mercy.

CONVERSATION STARTERS

When has sickness interfered with your plans?

When people help you, how do you thank them?

If Jesus visited your home and healed someone, how would you thank him?

WHERE TO FIND OUT MORE

Simon's Relative: Luke 4:38–40, Matthew 8:14–15, Mark 1:29–31

◇◇◇◇◇◇◇◇◇◇◇◇◇◇◇◇◇◇

A PRAYER

*Take a few silent moments. Imagine you are sick in bed,
and Jesus comes to visit. Is there something inside you
that needs healing right now? It might not be a physical hurt.
It could be something that hurts your heart, like mean words.
Imagine Jesus taking away your pain.
Let him hold your hand and look at you.
Thank Jesus for visiting, and close with an Amen.*

◇◇◇◇◇◇◇◇◇◇◇◇◇◇◇◇◇◇

DID SHE REMIND JESUS OF HIS MOM?

Jesus deeply cared about everyone he met, and he restored families many times. One day Jesus traveled to the little village of Nain, with a large crowd of people following him, and they met up with a sad group leaving the town with a dead body on a stretcher. They were on their way to bury the body. The dead person was a young man. His tearful mother walked behind her son's body. This probably felt like the darkest day of her life. Her only son was dead. In those days, a woman relied on a male relative to protect her and provide for her needs, and since her husband was also dead, she would be ignored without a male relative to speak on her behalf.

Jesus felt compassion for this woman. He knew someday his own mom would be grieving his death. It must have been painful for Jesus to witness such grief because he considers every family as his very own.

Jesus asked the funeral procession to stop. Jesus told the heartbroken mother not to cry. He touched the body on the stretcher and commanded the young man to get up. The dead son sat up and began to speak! Jesus had restored to the woman the only family she had left. The crowd gasped at the sight of such a marvelous miracle. People said that Jesus was a great prophet, right there in front of them! They recognized and said aloud that God was visiting them through Jesus.

Perhaps they remembered an ancient miracle recorded in their scriptures, when the prophet Elijah prayed in a city called Zarephath, and a widow's son recovered (1 Kings 17:17–24).

But Jesus was much more than a prophet. He was truly the Son of God. Reports about what Jesus had done spread throughout the whole area.

CONVERSATION STARTERS

How would you react if you heard that Jesus raised your friend back to life? Would you doubt the miracle and find some other explanation, or would you believe this fantastic story?

How might you bring healing to your family and friends?

Who in your neighborhood lives alone? What kindnesses could you do for them?

WHERE TO FIND OUT MORE

Widow's Son: Luke 7:11–17

Widow in Zarephath: 1 Kings 17:7–24

A PRAYER

Savior Jesus, you inspired Paul to tell the people in the church of Philippi to have no anxiety at all, but in every situation, to pray (Philippians 4:6). I come to you now with gratitude, and without fear. Please meet my family's needs. God, I wait for your peace. Amen.

SISTERS GET THEIR BROTHER BACK

Jesus loved Lazarus and his sisters so much that they were like his close relatives. So people wondered why Jesus didn't rush to see Lazarus when they told Jesus that Lazarus was terribly sick. Jesus kept the family waiting while he stayed a few more days in a distant city. By the time Jesus finally went to the town of Bethany where Lazarus lived, Lazarus had been dead and buried for four days. Lazarus's sister ran out to meet Jesus. She was upset that Jesus was late because she knew he could have saved her brother's life.

Jesus reminded her that anyone who believes in him will have eternal life. She understood and knew that Jesus would welcome us to heaven someday. She said, *"I have come to believe that you are the Messiah, the Son of God, the one who is coming into the world"* (John 11:27). But she did not yet realize that Jesus could bring dead people back to life.

Good Question!

What is a Messiah?

A Messiah is a leader and savior who rescues people from earthly troubles like war and poverty. The Jews did not understand that God as Messiah would come in the form of a person: Jesus. They thought that God would create an earthly kingdom, not a heavenly one that would last forever. It's important to know that Christ is not Jesus' last name. The word Christ means "Anointed One." The Jews expected God to anoint a leader to release them from suffering and start a powerful earthly kingdom. God had a different Messiah in mind.

When Jesus saw the tears of Lazarus's sister, he started crying too. The sorrow of the family touched his heart, even though he knew he was going to do something amazing. He asked to be shown where Lazarus was buried. What was he planning to do? People followed, wondering all the way.

Jesus said, *"Take away the stone"* (John 11:39).

Lazarus's sister knew that after someone dies, the physical body begins to decay, so she warned, *"Lord, by now there will be a stench; he has been dead for four days"* (John 11:39).

Jesus didn't respond to her. Instead, Jesus yelled, *"Lazarus, come out!"* (John 11:43). Lazarus emerged from the grave, still wrapped in burial cloths. Jesus asked the people to unwrap him.

Lazarus was alive!

Many more people who witnessed the miracle chose to agree with Lazarus's sister that Jesus is the Messiah and Son of God.

CONVERSATION STARTERS

When have you been so moved by someone else's tears, you started crying too?

How does crying with someone show that you care?

What does empathy mean to you?

WHERE TO FIND OUT MORE

Lazarus Returns from the Dead: John 11:1–48

◇◇◇◇◇◇◇◇◇◇◇◇◇◇◇◇◇◇◇◇◇◇

A PRAYER

*Take a few quiet moments. Imagine standing outside Lazarus's grave
with the sad crowd. Imagine hearing people sniffling and crying,
and Jesus and Lazarus's sister talking to each other.
Imagine smelling fresh grass, and maybe feeling warm sun.
Hear the stone scraping as people roll it away,
and imagine the gasps as a man
wrapped from head to toe comes out of the grave.
What would you like to say to Jesus?
Spend some time in silence. Finish with Amen.*

◇◇◇◇◇◇◇◇◇◇◇◇◇◇◇◇◇◇◇◇◇◇

Love one another as I love you.

—John 15:12

How Families Should Be

Jesus learned many lessons from his family life. Jesus wants us to know his heavenly Father, and he told a story to help us better understand how God acts toward us, his children. Jesus loved telling parables, and one that is quite well known involves a compassionate father whose family had some issues. The father was a great example of forgiveness.

Jesus' story of the prodigal son begins with the father's two children. One grew sick of living at home, and he knew that when his dad died, he would get a portion of everything, and the other portion would go to his brother. Disrespectfully, he asked his dad to give him his inheritance right away. The father generously gave the younger son what he asked for. The older son stayed home.

The younger son soon wasted all the money. Starving, he looked for work. The only job he could find was the messy task of tending pigs, an animal that the Jews considered ritually unclean. He got so hungry he wanted to eat the pigs' food. Coming to his senses, the son realized that his father treated his workers better than this. He decided to go home and apologize, and ask if his dad would hire him as a worker. He practiced what he would say when he came face-to-face with his dad.

Before the son got to the house, the father saw his beloved child returning and ran to greet him. Overjoyed, the father told the servants to prepare a big party. In telling the story, Jesus mentions no punishments. The father had already forgiven everything. (That's what Jesus does, too, by the way.)

Meanwhile, the older brother had been working hard in the fields. When he returned home and heard music playing, a servant explained that everyone was celebrating the return of his younger brother. The older brother was so furious, he refused to join the celebration. When the father heard this, he did not wait for this son to get over his anger. He went out to his son to talk, and to listen.

The older brother said, *"Look, all these years I served you and not once did I disobey your orders"* (Luke 15:29). He complained that never once had the dad thrown him a party. He was jealous, he was angry, and he wanted his brother punished.

The father replied: *"My son, you are here with me always; everything I have is yours. But now we must celebrate and rejoice, because your brother was dead and has come to life again; he was lost and has been found"* (Luke 15:31–32). Why? Because the brother had completely separated himself from the family. His return was like him coming back to life.

Jesus' story showed God's willingness to forgive everyone, even people who make bad choices. God eagerly welcomes anyone who expresses sorrow, no matter how long they've been away. And this parable explains that it's wrong to be jealous when others get good things they don't deserve. It reminds us not to point fingers at others. Only God has the authority to judge.

Families are a place to practice being like Jesus and forgiving each other by not holding on to pain. Jesus' story is a great guide for every family, including the one we call the Body of Christ. Jesus invites every human being to be part of this family.

CONVERSATION STARTERS

When was a time you felt jealousy toward someone else? Why?

What makes it difficult to admit being wrong?

Describe a time when you apologized.

WHERE TO FIND OUT MORE

The Prodigal Son: Luke 15:11–32

A PRAYER

Heavenly Father, I know sometimes I make poor choices.
I'm glad you forgive and heal. Thank you.
It's not easy for me to forgive others.
Please give me the grace to be more like you and to treat every person
as a member of Jesus' family—and mine. Amen.

[Jesus said,] *"It was not you who chose me,*

but I who chose you."

—John 15:16

PART 2:
JESUS AND HIS FRIENDS

Faithful friends are a sturdy shelter;

whoever finds one finds a treasure.

—*Sirach 6:14*

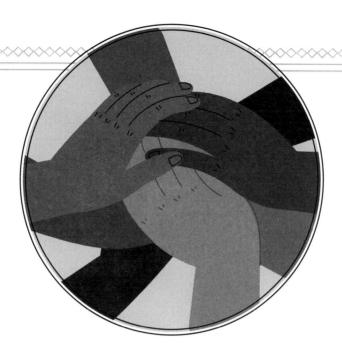

Many Kinds of Friends

Just as is true for you and me, the friends that Jesus made fall into different categories. Some people were acquaintances Jesus met in passing and did not have a chance to get to know very well. Some people became the kind of friends who were so interested in and drawn to Jesus, they were never the same after their first meeting. A few others became his most trusted followers, friends so close that Jesus entrusted them with his life and his life's work.

In this book, according to stories we read in the Gospels, we will arrange Jesus' friends into three groups: Apostles, disciples, and witnesses.

- *Apostles* were the twelve men chosen by Jesus to be his closest friends. Their names were Peter, Andrew, James, John, Phillip, Bartholomew, Thomas, Matthew, James, Thaddeus, Simon, and Judas (Matthew 10:1–8).

- *Disciples* followed Jesus closely and, like Apostles, they grew in their understanding of who Jesus is as both God and human.

- *Witnesses* met Jesus and expressed interest in knowing more about him.

Of course, it is difficult to put people into categories, and the Gospels only tell some of the stories of Jesus' friends. If every story of every friend of Jesus were written down, the whole world could not contain the books that these stories would fill (John 21:25).

Stories about Apostles

When Jesus began speaking and preaching in public about his message to love God and all people, he chose twelve men to be his Apostles. The reason Jesus chose twelve was because his ancestor, Israel, had twelve sons, whose descendants became known as the twelve tribes of Israel. As Jesus was unfolding God's plan, which was the fulfillment of the covenant he established with Abraham, Moses, and all the Israelites, Jesus wanted to include one Apostle for each of the twelve tribes. This would be a sign that Jesus is the fulfillment of God's agreement with all previous members of the Jewish family. Some of the Apostles were fishermen, some were tax collectors, and some were brothers.

JESUS CHOSE APOSTLES CAREFULLY

Jesus visited different places, including the Sea of Galilee, a large lake not far from where he lived, to invite people to join him in his work. The Sea of Galilee is a beautiful place, even today. Tall cliffs overlook it on one side, and flat plains end at the opposite shore. The lake is about thirty miles around, and about thirteen miles across at its widest point. The Sea of Galilee is the lowest freshwater lake on earth. It is surrounded by hills, which cause winds that can make the lake suddenly stormy.

Jesus watched four very frustrated fishermen who had been up all night fishing but hadn't caught even one fish! Meanwhile, people began pushing and shoving to get closer to Jesus to hear him speak. So Jesus asked a pair of brothers, Simon and Andrew, if he could borrow their boat. Simon agreed, and together they got in and pushed a short distance away from shore. Jesus spoke from the boat to the crowd. People listened with amazement.

Then Jesus told the brothers to try fishing again. Simon doubted this would work, but he did what Jesus suggested. Suddenly the net was so full of fish that the brothers could not lift it! They signaled to their partners James and John, another pair of brothers, to help them.

Working as hard as they could, they filled both boats with fish until they almost sank from the weight. Everyone was astounded.

Jesus invited these four fishermen to join him as Apostles, saying that from now on they'd be catching people instead of fish. How strange and mysterious! Would they collect them in nets? No. Jesus would use timeless parables, healings, and miracles to show his followers how to "catch" people up in a "net" of God's love. The Apostles would have special roles leading people to know, love, and serve God.

Simon felt unworthy to accept Jesus' invitation. He even suggested that Jesus leave without him. Jesus knew that Simon had shortcomings, but Jesus loved him just as he was. Jesus reassured Simon that nobody is perfect. Later, Jesus gave Simon a new name: Peter, which means "rock." Peter would become the first pope, a "rock" on which Jesus built the Church.

The brothers immediately left everything behind and started a new life traveling with Jesus.

The new Apostles, brothers Peter and Andrew and brothers James and John, asked questions, listened, learned, and became four of Jesus' closest friends.

CONVERSATION STARTERS

What makes it easy for siblings to be friends?

Do you have any nicknames? If Jesus gave you a nickname, what do you imagine it would be?

WHERE TO FIND OUT MORE

Jesus Calls Brothers: Matthew 4:18–22 and Luke 5:1–11

A PRAYER

Take a few slow breaths and close your eyes. Imagine being at the Sea of Galilee the day Jesus called these brothers. Watch the men drop everything to follow Jesus. Imagine being their dad, Zebedee, or a younger sibling. How do you feel? Do you want to join them? Is Jesus smiling at you? What might you say to Jesus? Take some silent time. Finish with Amen.

APOSTLES HIKE WITH JESUS

Jesus chose three close friends, Peter, James, and John, to join him on a hike. When they reached the mountaintop, something remarkable happened. Jesus suddenly started to glow with a bright light. Two important people, Moses and Elijah, appeared and started talking with Jesus—these leaders of Israel had been dead for hundreds of years! They were also glowing. Clearly, Jesus was connected to God. And he wanted his close friends to be present for this incredible conversation.

Imagine how Jesus' friends reacted when they saw Jesus talking to long-dead leaders, all of them glowing with bright light. When Peter offered to build tents for them all, he really had no idea what he was saying. It must have been difficult for the Apostles to understand that all holy people who have died, including those who died before Jesus was born, are alive with God now.

Then a bright cloud came down, and it cast an enormous shadow. The Apostles heard a powerful voice coming from it, saying that Jesus is God's beloved son, and they should listen to Jesus.

Terrified, the Apostles fell to the ground and hid their eyes. The next thing they knew, Jesus was telling them to get up, and when they did, Jesus was alone, looking normal again. Jesus trusted and valued these Apostles so much that he wanted them to know more about who he truly was. Jesus asked Peter, James, and John not to tell anyone what had happened on the mountain until after Jesus came back to life—that is, after his resurrection from the dead. And, being trustworthy friends, they kept what happened just between them.

CONVERSATION STARTERS

Do you treasure your friends and share special moments with them, as Jesus did on the mountain?

Why do you think Jesus allowed his friends to watch his meeting with some important people from heaven?

WHERE TO FIND OUT MORE

Transfiguration: Matthew 17:1–9 and Luke 9:28–36

⬦⬦⬦⬦⬦⬦⬦⬦⬦⬦⬦⬦⬦⬦⬦⬦⬦⬦⬦

A PRAYER

Comforting Jesus, thank you for revealing so many truths about friendship.
Sometimes I hide the real me. Help me trust that you will always accept me,
no matter what I think, say, or do.
Thank you for always being my friend. Amen.

⬦⬦⬦⬦⬦⬦⬦⬦⬦⬦⬦⬦⬦⬦⬦⬦⬦⬦⬦

JESUS IS BETRAYED BY AN APOSTLE

Whenever Jesus visited Jerusalem, he liked going to the Garden of Gethsemane on the Mount of Olives with his friends. Judas, who was one of the Apostles, decided to use this knowledge against him. Judas secretly asked the priests of the temple how much money they would give him if he led soldiers to Jesus so that they could arrest him. Those scheming against Jesus were happy to pay Judas to betray his friend.

The plotters feared that Jesus' supporters would get angry and riot if Jesus was arrested in daylight, so they decided to sneak up on Jesus at night. Since it would be so dark the guards might have trouble telling the difference between Jesus and his friends, Judas used a secret signal: a kiss.

Good Question!

Why would a kiss be a secret signal?

In Jesus' day, a kiss was like a handshake. Even today you may see people greet friends by pressing their cheeks together and kissing the air.

The evening of the Last Supper arrived. Judas had made all the arrangements. He waited for an opportunity to slink out early. Throughout the feast, Jesus was solemn. He knew that one of the Apostles would betray him, and he told them so.

What? His friends became very upset. Jesus had already foreseen enough events that they knew they could trust his prediction. Each worried that he might betray Jesus by accident. But Jesus looked straight at Judas and said that if he was going to do something, to do it quickly. And Judas did not stick around. He wasted no time in fetching the guards who would arrest Jesus.

After they finished eating, Jesus and his friends walked to their special garden. Because he was also God, Jesus knew what was going to happen, and he expressed deep sadness.

Jesus asked his best friends to stay close by and to pray. He stepped away for a bit of privacy, and he prayed hard—so hard that his sweat became like drops of blood dripping down his face. Do you know what his friends did? They fell asleep. That must have hurt Jesus' feelings.

Since Jesus was fully human, he suffered that night in the garden.

Good Question!

Sometimes I feel like I have no friends.
Did Jesus ever feel that way?

Yes. While on the cross, Jesus felt horrible. He spoke words from Psalm 22 that describe feeling abandoned. By immediately praying, Jesus demonstrated what to do when we feel down. It's good to feel the feelings but we should not get stuck in them. Jesus told God how he felt, knowing his Father could take whatever we have to say. Jesus resisted the temptation to despair. He prayed the rest of Psalm 22 which transitions to a prayer of gratitude. Gratitude is a secret weapon when feeling bad. Your feelings may not change immediately. Thank God anyway and be patient. God will give you either a way out or the strength to endure. Either way, we are never alone in our time of sorrow. God is with us.

Meanwhile, Judas led the soldiers to the garden at the Mount of Olives. Jesus could see them creeping up as if he were a criminal. When Judas kissed Jesus, the guards knew who to put under arrest.

Jesus did not interfere with Judas's free choice to turn him in for money, even though he was very hurt by one of his best friends.

CONVERSATION STARTERS

When has a friend disappointed you?

Has someone ever stopped being your friend? How did it make you feel? What did you do?

Even though Jesus knew Judas would betray him, Jesus continued being a friend to him. Why do you think Jesus did this?

WHERE TO FIND OUT MORE

Judas Betrays Jesus: Luke 22:1–6, 21–23, 47–51; Matthew 26:14–16, 20–25, 47–50; Mark 14:18–20, 43–46; and John 18:1–9

◇◇◇◇◇◇◇◇◇◇◇◇◇◇◇◇◇◇

A PRAYER

Patient Jesus, I don't know how you endured such suffering.
You knew that God's plan to save the world from sin involved suffering.
That's hard for me to understand.
I know I don't have to understand everything because, after all, I am not you.
But I ask for faith to believe that you will always be with me when I suffer.
You understand how deeply people can hurt us.
Jesus, I will trust you. Amen.

◇◇◇◇◇◇◇◇◇◇◇◇◇◇◇◇◇◇◇◇◇

Stories about Disciples

Disciples were people eager to share in Jesus' mission and to imitate him. Many women became disciples of Jesus as he moved from place to place, cooking and buying supplies to support him and the twelve Apostles as they traveled around teaching and healing. Among the friends Jesus made while traveling were some who joined his journeys. Others stayed home and lived lives that were holier because of what they had experienced with Jesus.

TWO SISTERS FOLLOW JESUS IN DIFFERENT WAYS

As Jesus traveled to various towns, he made friends everywhere he went. In one village he was welcomed into the home of Martha, whose sister Mary lived there also. Martha quickly got to work preparing a meal for the guests, but Mary didn't help. Instead, Mary sat at Jesus' feet so that she could hear every word he said.

Have you ever felt like you were doing all the work and one of your siblings or classmates wasn't doing anything? If so, then you understand how Martha felt.

Martha was preoccupied with all she had to do. She felt upset that Mary wasn't doing any chores, so she went to Jesus and complained. It seemed to her that Jesus didn't care that Mary had left her to do all the serving. Martha asked Jesus to tell Mary to help!

But Jesus said, *"Martha, Martha, you are anxious and worried about many things"* (Luke 10:41). Jesus understood how Martha felt. However, at that moment, Mary was doing the better thing.

Sometimes we need to be reminded that worrying is a waste of time. The better thing to do is to take a few moments to pray. Jesus gently told Martha the truth. Friendship involves being honest, even if that means pointing out someone's mistakes.

CONVERSATION STARTERS

What do you think Martha chose to do? Do you think she sat down with Mary and listened to Jesus?

Do you think Jesus helped both of the women with the chores after he finished speaking?

Describe a time when you felt worried or anxious. What helped you find peace?

WHERE TO FIND OUT MORE

Martha and Mary: Luke 10:38–42 and John 12:2

◇◇◇◇◇◇◇◇◇◇◇◇◇◇◇◇◇◇◇◇◇◇

A PRAYER

Understanding Jesus, speak to me today.
Let me listen as if I am sitting at your feet. Take away worries.
You said that fear is useless. And worry is a kind of fear.
Thank you for caring about how I feel. Amen.

◇◇◇◇◇◇◇◇◇◇◇◇◇◇◇◇◇◇◇◇◇◇◇◇

MEETING JESUS CHANGED HIS LIFE

Zacchaeus, a wealthy man who happened to be very short, lived in Jericho and worked for the Roman government as the chief tax collector. Jewish leaders considered Zacchaeus a sinner.

One day, Zacchaeus heard someone shouting, "Jesus is coming! Jesus is coming!" Excited to see the man he'd heard so much about, Zacchaeus ran outside. But the road was already crowded and he couldn't see over the tall people. Did he give up? No. He climbed a tree. He didn't care about his nice clothes or what people might think. He wanted to see Jesus.

And Jesus wanted to see him. *When he reached the place, Jesus looked up and said to him, "Zacchaeus, come down quickly, for today I must stay at your house"* (Luke 19:5). Zacchaeus must have wondered how Jesus already knew his name.

Overjoyed, Zacchaeus scrambled down that tree as fast as his short legs could take him. But others shook their heads. Why would Jesus choose to go to Zacchaeus's house? That tax collector was bad news! But Jesus saw something different. He saw that Zacchaeus could change his life. This was another instance where Jesus was making an important point: God loves all human beings, no matter their reputation.

Zacchaeus felt excited that Jesus had invited himself over. He never expected such an honor. As a result of Jesus' visit, Zacchaeus decided to live generously. He told Jesus he would give half of everything he had to people who were poor. He also promised to pay back four times the amount to everyone he had cheated. Jesus applauded Zacchaeus's decisions, saying, *"Today salvation has come to this house because this man too is a descendant of Abraham"* (Luke 19:9).

By calling him a *"descendant of Abraham,"* Jesus demonstrated that Zacchaeus belonged to the family of God. Jesus rejoiced to see Zacchaeus's change of heart. Jesus came *"to seek and to save what was lost"* (Luke 19:10).

CONVERSATION STARTERS

Describe a time when someone questioned you for being friends with someone else who didn't fit in.

How important are clothes, hairstyles, and jobs? How do they affect how people are treated?

Zacchaeus changed his life to better follow Jesus' ways. What in your world would you like to see changed?

WHERE TO FIND OUT MORE

Zacchaeus: Luke 19:1–10

Jesus Eats with Sinners: Mark 2:13–17

Jesus Calls Another Tax Collector: Matthew 9:9–13

A PRAYER

Understanding Jesus, you are full of surprises.
You make friends with interesting and unusual people.
Help me accept people who are different from me.
When I hear something shocking about a friend,
help me not gossip or say something mean or insulting.
I want to be kind always. Thank you for hearing my prayer. Amen.

DISCIPLES SEE GREAT POWER

The sun was setting. Huge crowds had walked long distances to get a glimpse of Jesus, to hear him, and maybe have a chance to speak with him. Jesus wove together wonderful stories about seeds and plants, about caring for others, and about doing good deeds. Jesus loved telling parables, but now he was tired because he'd been talking all day, and it was getting dark. Jesus invited his disciples to cross to the other side of the lake. His friends took him into their boat and began to row to the opposite shore. Tired as he was, Jesus quickly fell asleep.

A violent storm arose without warning. Waves crashed so high, the boat began taking on water. Still Jesus slept.

His friends trembled in fear. How could Jesus be sleeping? They wondered if Jesus cared at all whether everyone would be drowned that very night.

They woke him to ask for his help. Jesus immediately commanded the raging storm to be quiet. At once, the wind stopped. Instantly, the wild sea calmed. Everyone was amazed to see that even the wind and sea obeyed Jesus.

When the danger had passed, Jesus asked his friends why they were terrified. After all the miracles they had seen, didn't they trust him?

CONVERSATION STARTERS

If you were in the boat during this adventure, how would you have felt? What would you have done?

How can you trust in Jesus at the same time as you are feeling afraid?

Every life has "stormy seas" from time to time. How can people grow in trusting God?

WHERE TO FIND OUT MORE

Jesus Calms a Storm: Mark 4:35–41, Matthew 8:23–27, and Luke 8:22–25

A PRAYER

Kind friend Jesus, sometimes I feel afraid. I get worried.
You said many times that we have no need to fear.
Please help me trust in you. Give me courage when frightening things happen.
I know that you always care. Amen.

JESUS SHOWS THE WAY TO JOY

The road sloped gently down from Jerusalem as two disciples of Jesus with heavy hearts trudged away from the city. Jesus was buried days ago. The Sabbath was over. The disciples saw no reason to stay in Jerusalem any longer.

As they walked, heads lowered, a man approached them. The two travelers invited the stranger to walk along with them. The man asked what they were talking about. They stopped in their tracks; they had been talking about Jesus. One of the travelers said that this man must be the only person in Jerusalem who didn't know what had just happened there.

Now, the truth is that the man who had joined the two travelers was Jesus, but they did not recognize Jesus' resurrected body.

Jesus chose to let them explain everything about how Jesus was arrested, tortured, and killed by crucifixion. The disciples explained that on the third day after Jesus' death, some women shocked them by reporting that they had seen angels making an announcement that Jesus was alive again.

They added that others ran to the tomb. They, too, found it empty. But these two disciples had seen no evidence that their friend had returned to life. They had left town feeling discouraged and downcast.

When they finished recounting the whole story, Jesus responded by unraveling all the clues in the Bible that pointed to a suffering servant who would save all people, not just the nation of Israel. As Jesus talked, their sadness began to lift. Soon, the two friends felt enthusiastic about the fulfillment of God's plans.

When they reached their destination, which was Emmaus, the two asked their traveling companion to stay. He did.

When the three sat down to eat, Jesus took the bread, said the blessing, broke it, and gave it to them. With that their eyes were opened, and they realized that this was Jesus!

We, too, recognize Jesus in the Eucharist we celebrate and receive at Mass.

The moment the two recognized him, Jesus vanished. The disciples decided to hurry back to Jerusalem. They couldn't wait to tell the others that they had seen Jesus alive again.

Back in Jerusalem, the disciples heard surprising news: Jesus also had been to see the Apostles! The travelers recounted how Jesus had revealed himself by breaking bread, and as they described their walk to Emmaus with Jesus, they realized that what they felt building up inside them was joy and hope.

CONVERSATION STARTERS

When have you been with someone who lifted your spirits so much that you didn't want them to leave?

Who cheers you up when you need encouragement? Could Jesus be using someone you know as a sort of "disguise?"

How can you grow in paying attention to your heart, and recognize when God's love fills it?

WHERE TO FIND OUT MORE

Emmaus: Luke 24:13–35

Suffering Servant: Isaiah 52:13—53:12

◇◇◇◇◇◇◇◇◇◇◇◇◇◇◇◇◇◇◇◇◇

A PRAYER

Take a few quiet moments. Imagine that you are walking along that road
with the disciples, and Jesus starts walking alongside you.
Imagine that he is explaining the meaning of Scripture.
How does your heart feel?
After a few silent moments,
conclude your meditation with Amen.

◇◇◇◇◇◇◇◇◇◇◇◇◇◇◇◇◇◇◇◇◇

Stories about Witnesses

Jesus relied on friends to help him during his time on earth. He chose a variety of friends from among ordinary people, poor people, unpopular people, and hurting people. You might think he would start with rich and powerful people. He didn't. Those he chose reacted in different ways. Here are some examples of what people did when they got to know Jesus.

JESUS BEFRIENDS OUTSIDERS

Jesus came to a town in Samaria, and he was really tired, so he sat down on the edge of a well while his friends went into town to find food. While he was sitting there, a woman came to the well to get water to take home. What happened next demonstrated just how much Jesus was against every kind of prejudice.

Jesus asked the woman for a drink. She put down her jars and gave him a funny look. She thought he must be kidding. Jews typically avoided interacting with Samaritans whom they saw as unclean. She reminded him that it was considered impolite for men to start conversations with women they didn't know.

But Jesus kept talking, and he said that if she knew who he was, *she* would have asked *him* for "living water."

She scoffed. "You don't even have a bucket! This well is extremely deep! How in the world do you think you can give *me* any kind of water?" And she put her foot on the edge of the well to steady herself as she drew up some water. Jesus began telling her many details about her life, details that a stranger would have no way of knowing. His knowledge about her and his wisdom convinced the woman that he must be a prophet.

When Jesus' friends came back from town with food, they were very surprised to see him talking to a Samaritan, and a woman at that. She did not speak to them; she simply picked up her water jars and rushed home, where she told everyone in town that she had met the Messiah. By doing this, she became a witness to how Jesus welcomed everyone to be friends with him, even people he didn't know. She encouraged people to come and see for themselves that Jesus was open to getting to know people regardless of any label.

None of Jesus' friends asked him why he was talking to the woman. Perhaps they were beginning to understand that Jesus came to love everyone, no exceptions.

CONVERSATION STARTERS

Do you remember a time someone important or popular surprised you by turning their attention to you and talking to you? How did you feel?

Why do you think this woman decided to talk to Jesus? She didn't even know him.

Do you think that Jesus' friends instantly gave up their prejudices against Samaritans after this? What do you think happened in their hearts and minds as a result of this encounter?

WHERE TO FIND OUT MORE

Woman at the Well: John 4:5–42

◇◇◇◇◇◇◇◇◇◇◇◇◇◇◇◇◇◇◇◇◇◇◇◇

A PRAYER

Loving Mother Mary, your son often surprises me.
Will you ask him to help me love people who are different from me?
It is sometimes hard for me to be accepting of people who are different from me.
Thank you for hearing my prayer. Amen.

◇◇◇◇◇◇◇◇◇◇◇◇◇◇◇◇◇◇◇◇◇◇◇◇

FRIENDS SEEK AND WITNESS A MIRACLE

People packed the house. Listeners blocked the doorway. In Capernaum, a city on Galilee's seashore, Jesus welcomed all kinds of people, including some with big questions and some who were very sick.

Four friends wanted Jesus to see their pal who couldn't walk, but they couldn't get into the crowded house. The clever friends climbed onto the roof, and pulled their friend up! Imagine how that must have felt for the paralyzed friend! The friends then made a hole in the roof and lowered their friend down on a stretcher so that he could meet Jesus.

Jesus appreciated the effort these friends made for the paralyzed person. Many times in his life, Jesus relied on the help and companionship of his friends, so he understood and approved of friends caring for each other.

Jesus saw that they really believed he had the power to heal, and he saw how strong their friendships were. Seeing their faith, Jesus told the paralytic that his sins were forgiven.

What a surprise! Some in the crowd sneered. How dare Jesus say he can forgive sins! Only God can do that. They did not believe Jesus was God.

Knowing their thoughts, Jesus challenged those mocking him by asking if it was easier to forgive someone, or to heal someone who couldn't walk. The disbelievers didn't know what to say. Not waiting for an answer, Jesus told the paralyzed friend to get up, pick up his mat, and go home. And the friend stood, completely healed.

Gasps filled the room. Never had anyone done anything like this before. Through these actions Jesus showed that he *did* have the ability and the right to forgive sins. Jesus valued the friends' loyalty and determination to get their friend cured. They were witnesses to Jesus' authority.

CONVERSATION STARTERS

The Bible doesn't say if the healed person went home or not. What do you imagine happened next? What would you have done if it were you?

Is there someone you want to bring to Jesus for healing? Do you need healing from something?

Do you have any images of Jesus in your house? Consider printing a piece of artwork from the web to remind you that Jesus is part of your family.

WHERE TO FIND OUT MORE

Jesus Heals a Paralyzed Man: Mark 2:1–12

A PRAYER

Imagine that you are sitting in church one Sunday when Jesus walks in and sits down beside you. What would you say to him?
"Hello? What are you doing here?" Or maybe you'd ask him a question.
Imagine Jesus saying something to you right now.
(Among other things, Jesus is telling you that he loves you.) If you feel anxious about anything, tell Jesus. He is famous for giving us a sense of peace.
Imagine that Jesus is holding your hand. After a few quiet moments, thank God for this time with Jesus. Close with Amen.

GRATITUDE SHOWN IN TEARS

The Bible includes many passages about Jesus eating with groups of friends and acquaintances. Some were grateful for his messages and some were not.

Once while Jesus was eating at Simon the Pharisee's house, a woman came in and cried tears that fell onto Jesus' feet. Everyone in town knew about her bad behavior, and Simon suspected that if Jesus didn't know about her reputation, he must not be a very good prophet. Jesus knew what Simon was thinking! So he decided to explain something important to someone Jesus hoped would become his friend.

Good Question!

What is a Pharisee?

The Jewish faith had many leaders. Some, especially the Pharisees, were extremely strict about following ancient rules, and were known for being boastful and proud. They felt that following rules made them holier than other people.

Jesus asked Simon to imagine two people who owed money. Both people were told that they would not have to repay the debt. Jesus asked Simon who would be more grateful: The person who didn't have to repay $25 or the one who didn't have to repay $500. Simon said the person who didn't have to repay the larger amount would be more grateful. Then Jesus explained his response to the woman weeping at his feet. He saw the woman's deep sorrow and desire to change. He saw that her sins caused her pain. She showed tremendous gratitude because Jesus forgave all her many sins. Jesus explained that she felt great love because she had been forgiven so much.

Some dinner guests were not convinced. They wondered who Jesus thought he was to be forgiving sins. And since they didn't think of themselves as great sinners, they were not grateful for his explanation.

CONVERSATION STARTERS

When have you felt the weight of something so bad that you could cry? How did Jesus comfort you?

How has Jesus used family members or friends to help you feel forgiven?

When have you felt grateful because you were forgiven?

WHERE TO FIND OUT MORE

Jesus Is Anointed: Luke 7:36–47

Jesus Knocks: Revelation 3:20

A PRAYER

Take a few quiet moments to imagine Jesus outside your door, knocking.
How does Jesus knock? Do you hear a gentle tapping or
an insistent rapping on the door?
Now imagine that Jesus calls your name,
and you recognize his voice, so you open the door.
Jesus comes in and asks if he can stay for dinner. "Of course!" you say.
"But we're only having leftovers." Jesus says he doesn't mind.
He simply wants to be with you.
Take some time listening to Jesus. End with a prayer
in your own words and an Amen.

NOT EVERYONE LIKED JESUS

Not everyone who met Jesus wanted him as a friend. When he revisited Nazareth, where he grew up, some people got so angry that they tried to throw Jesus off a cliff. This happened after he read aloud from the Bible in the synagogue. The passage referred to God's anointed one, who would bring good news to people who were poor.

After Jesus read, everyone stared at him, waiting for him to talk about what the reading meant.

Jesus announced that he was God's chosen one, the Messiah.

While some expressed amazement, others remained doubtful. They knew his father, the craftsman and carpenter in town. How could Jesus be the one sent by God? He seemed so ordinary—a man like anyone else. Who did he think he was? God's spirit was in *him*?

Jesus knew what they thought, and he wasn't surprised. He reminded them that many times before, the very people God wanted to reach rejected prophets. This only made Jesus' audience angrier. That's when some people tried to throw him off a hill.

Jesus just walked right past them and moved on to make other friends in other places.

Time passed. Jesus kept sharing his new ideas about God, and some people couldn't believe him. For example, when Jesus explained that he himself is living bread, and we would eat his body in communion, and those who eat of his flesh will live forever, some people refused to accept this, and even some good friends walked away.

And Jesus let them. He asked his closest friends if they wanted to leave too, because Jesus insisted that he *is* bread for salvation. This was no parable or pretend example. This was truth, even if it sounded shocking. If his friends didn't want to accept it, Jesus said they were free to walk away. He invited people but never pushed them to do what was right.

Nobody is forced to follow Jesus.

Peter spoke up, saying that he and the others were convinced that Jesus is truly God's only son, and that Jesus' words lead to eternal life in heaven.

Peter was right.

CONVERSATION STARTERS

Why do you think that not everyone likes Jesus?

What do you have trouble believing?

Who answers your questions about God?

WHERE TO FIND OUT MORE

What Jesus Reads in the Synagogue: Isaiah 61:1–6

Jesus Is Rejected: Luke 4:14–30

Friends Leave: John 6:27–69

A PRAYER

Jesus, you are the Son of God, the Bread of Life, our Savior, brother, and friend. When I have doubts, help me to be like those friends who stuck with you even when their faith was weak. Thanks. Amen.

A CRIMINAL DEFENDS JESUS

The Skull Place. That was the hill just outside of Jerusalem where Romans crucified people. Romans chose a busy road for their torturous killings so that travelers coming and going from the important city would see dying criminals and be warned to obey the laws.

Jesus carried his cross to the Skull Place, known as Golgotha in Aramaic, which was the language that Jesus spoke. There, he was nailed to the cross and put on display for anyone to see. But first they stripped off his clothes and threw dice among the soldiers to see who would get them. Death from public and humiliating torture might make a person angry and hateful. Not Jesus. He forgave people who others thought didn't deserve it.

As Jesus was dying on the cross, he asked God the Father to forgive everyone involved in his death—even the soldiers who sneered and the bystanders who laughed at his suffering. Jesus even forgave a man dying on a cross next to him. One of the two convicts hanging on either side of Jesus made fun of him. But the other reminded the cruel criminal that the two of them deserved punishment because they were guilty. But Jesus had done nothing wrong. This guilty man asked a favor of Jesus: *"Jesus, remember me when you come into your kingdom"* (Luke 23:42), meaning when Jesus went to heaven. Jesus said, *"Today you will be with me in Paradise"* (Luke 23:43). No matter what the man's crimes were, Jesus forgave them all.

This story in the Bible is a powerful witness statement. It is never too late to become Jesus' friend.

CONVERSATION STARTERS

Why do you want to choose Jesus as your friend?

Who is someone who encourages you when you feel down?

How might you witness that you are Jesus' friend?

WHERE TO FIND OUT MORE

A Good Thief Gives Witness: Luke 23:32–43

◇◇◇◇◇◇◇◇◇◇◇◇◇◇◇◇◇◇◇◇

A PRAYER

Today I chose you as my leader and friend.
I know I will make mistakes,
but I also know you will always accept me,
no matter what. Amen.

◇◇◇◇◇◇◇◇◇◇◇◇◇◇◇◇◇◇◇◇

You are precious in my eyes and honored,

and I love you [says the Lord].

—Isaiah 43:4

"You Are My Friends." Yes, YOU!

Jesus said, *"You are my friends"* (John 15:14). Isn't it a mystery that Jesus, who is one of the three persons of the Holy Trinity and already has everything, wants our friendship?

How can ordinary human beings be friends with an invisible God who created everything, who is a pure Holy Spirit, and Jesus risen from the dead?

When we treat any person as a friend, Jesus sees that as a friendship with himself because God lives in every human heart! When we decide to be God's friends, something amazing happens. Jesus works through us to make the world better.

One of the witnesses to Jesus, Teresa of Ávila, a Doctor of the Church, put it this way:

> Christ has no body but yours; no hands, no feet on earth but yours.
> Yours are the eyes with which He looks with compassion on
>   this world.
> Yours are the feet with which He walks to do good.
> Yours are the hands with which He blesses all the world.

Good Question!

What is a Doctor of the Church?

Over the centuries, the Church has given the title "Doctor of the Church" to 37 saints. This means they studied, wrote, or in some way contributed to important conversations about God. And their ideas help us better understand our faith. Teresa of Ávila, a Spanish Carmelite who experienced spiritual visions, wrote such beautiful books about God that she became the first woman Doctor of the Church.

Jesus is working through you, and sees you as a friend no matter what. Jesus doesn't love you because *you* are good. Jesus loves you because *God* is good. Even when you don't believe in yourself, God believes in you. Jesus wants us to know that we are very important to God, no matter how small our lives might seem, and whether or not we do well in school, or whether we have a disability, or we have a family that isn't very loving. Jesus wants to be friends with everybody. No exceptions. And he never gives up reaching out to make new friends.

Jesus always draws us gently into making the most loving choices. Love shares many qualities with friendship. The Apostle Paul, in his letter to people living in Corinth, said that love is patient, kind, gentle, and peaceable. The same is true of friendship.

It bears all things, believes all things, hopes all things, endures all things. Love never fails (1 Corinthians 13:7–8).

As Sister Ida Peterfy, a witness to Jesus who in 1940 started a community called the Sisters of the Society Devoted to the Sacred Heart of Jesus, put it, "Because you can talk to God, something very, very special can happen: you can have a friendship with God!"

CONVERSATION STARTERS

When have you been able to recognize God's love and friendship in another person's behavior?

How might you be Jesus' hands by doing some act of kindness for someone?

WHERE TO FIND OUT MORE

What Love Is and Isn't: 1 Corinthians 13:4–8

You Are My Friends: John 15:12–17

◇◇◇◇◇◇◇◇◇◇◇◇◇◇◇◇◇◇

A PRAYER

Kind Jesus, thank you for saying you want us to be friends,
and that loving others is the way to be friends with you. I want to.
But when people aren't very nice, help me follow your example,
and help me get better at forgiving. Thank you. Amen.

◇◇◇◇◇◇◇◇◇◇◇◇◇◇◇◇◇◇

Therefore, encourage one another

and build one another up.

—1 Thessalonians 5:11

PART 3:
JESUS AND FRIENDSHIP

Be kind to one another,

compassionate, forgiving one another

as God has forgiven you in Christ.

—*Ephesians 4:32*

Friendship
Involves
Compassion

Friendship is very important to Jesus, who wants the best for every human being. Someone once asked Jesus what it means to be friends with God. Jesus replied that we must love our neighbors as we love ourselves. But the person asking the question asked another: Who is my neighbor? Jesus answered with a story about a traveler who was beaten, robbed, and left for dead on the side of the road.

A Jewish priest came along after the attack and noticed the wounded person, but crossed the road to avoid him. A second traveler, a temple official, reacted the same way. Then along came a Samaritan.

The Samaritan felt compassion and bandaged the stranger, lifted him onto his donkey, and took him to an inn. He paid for lodgings and food so that the wounded traveler could rest and recover for as many days as needed. The Samaritan told the innkeeper to take care of the hurting traveler, and promised to pay the costs of his care when he returned.

Now, that was mercy.

The people who were listening to Jesus tell this story surely were surprised to hear that the hero was a Samaritan. Many Jews thought that Samaritans weren't as faithful to God as *they* were. Jesus wanted to end prejudice. And so, Jesus asked everyone to consider which of the three people on the road that day acted in a spirit of true friendship and did the right thing. The answer, of course, was the man who treated the wounded traveler with mercy. The Samaritan.

Jesus said that whatever we do for people in need is something we do for him. Every positive action improves our friendship with Jesus, who lives inside of everyone, whether they know it or not. This is because God is everywhere, and can be recognized in all things.

CONVERSATION STARTERS

How does your family reach out to help people who suffer injustice?

Talk with your family and friends about things you can do to help people in need.

Are there people you are uncomfortable with because they are different from you? How was the dislike that some Jews had for Samaritans in Jesus' day a form of racism?

WHERE TO FIND OUT MORE

Parable of the Good Samaritan: Luke 10:25–37

God Judges Nations: Matthew 25:31–40

Love Your Neighbor as Yourself: Leviticus 19:18

Being Kind to the Needy Is a Blessing: Proverbs 14:21

Love Your Enemies: Matthew 5:43–48

A PRAYER

Holy Spirit, sometimes I can be mean to certain people.
Help me avoid this sin. I want to be like the Good Samaritan.
Your story shows that every time I am kind to someone,
I am being kind to you. Please help me act with compassion.
Thank you for hearing my prayer. Amen.

[Jesus said,] *"But to you who hear I say,*

love your enemies,

do good to those who hate you."

—*Luke 6:27*

Friendship Means Loving Even Enemies

Jesus took every opportunity to show that loving everyone is important to him. The story of how the tax collector Matthew became an Apostle is an example. One day, Jesus looked straight at Matthew and said, *"Follow me"* (Matthew 9:9), and Matthew did, right then and there. Matthew then threw a party for Jesus. He invited his tax collector friends as well as people with bad reputations. Jesus didn't mind. He hoped to become friends with everyone. Jesus urged these people to be good and to stay away from things that might tempt them to sin.

Meanwhile, important men in the religious community complained that Jesus was hanging out with their enemies. Tax collectors were the wrong crowd; many Jewish people considered them traitors because they worked for the Romans, who charged people too much for taxes. The religious men thought that Jesus should be friends only with people who were respected in the community. They did not understand that God loves all people, even when they sin. Jesus described himself as a doctor. People don't seek a doctor if they think there's nothing wrong with them. Jesus knew that people whose hearts were unhealthy needed his attention. Jesus wanted the leaders to stop criticizing and to realize that they needed his doctoring, too! God is all merciful and loving—to everyone.

The leaders shook their heads. They wanted to make sure people were punished for their sins. Jesus wanted to be friends with these men, too, but many of them judged him to be not holy enough, and not religious enough by their standards. In their eyes he was a rule breaker. They chose not to be associated with Jesus and his circle of friends.

Matthew understood that Jesus wanted to heal people and bring them together, which is why Matthew left his job. He then gave his life to imitating Jesus, eventually becoming one of Jesus' dearest friends. Matthew's experiences as Jesus' friend are the basis of the Gospel named for this former tax collector.

Jesus also helped unpopular Roman guards. One guard showed such great faith in Jesus' power that Jesus used him as a powerful example. The guard sent a message to Jesus saying, *"Lord, I am not worthy to have you enter under my roof; only say the word and my servant will be healed"* (Matthew 8:8). He meant that Jesus didn't even have to come to his house because Jesus' word alone could heal. Jesus indeed spoke words of healing without going to the Roman's house, and the servant was cured.

Romans? Pharisees? Jews? Samaritans? No matter who we are and how we are known and identified, Jesus showed that he wants everyone to love one another.

CONVERSATION STARTERS

Do you recognize the words the Roman guard said to Jesus? When do we use similar words at Mass?

What might you do when your friends argue with or dislike one other?

When have you reached out in friendship to someone who is unpopular?

WHERE TO FIND OUT MORE

Follow Me: Matthew 9:9–13

Jesus Wants to Call Sinners: Luke 5:27–32

The Centurion's Servant: Matthew 8:5–13 and Luke 7:1–10

A PRAYER

Healing Jesus, please help people whose friendships are broken,
and help me to love people who are different from me.
Help us to see goodness in everyone.
Heal those needing relief from pain or sadness.
Unite us all in love. Thanks! Amen.

Let love be sincere; hate what is evil,

hold on to what is good; love one another

with mutual affection;

anticipate one another in showing honor.

—Romans 12:9–10

Friendship May Involve Challenging Someone

It can be hard to be brave and act when you see something wrong, especially when it involves a friend making unwise choices.

One day, Jesus walked into the temple to pray with some friends. There, right in the holy place, people had tables full of things for sale, including oxen and sheep! Can you imagine going to Mass and finding people selling cupcakes, video games, and pets *inside* the church? Would you dare to say something about it?

Jesus did. He flipped over the sellers' tables. Whatever was on them scattered everywhere. Then he drove the animals out of the temple. Jesus sure got everyone's attention. It was clear that he was displeased with the way people were treating God's house.

Everywhere he went, Jesus made a big impression on people who did wrong. He pointed out that money and power can tempt people to evil. It was no surprise that people who valued money and power more than they valued their relationship with God began to plot against Jesus.

Jesus' example challenges us to take daring action for God, too. Is there any kind of brave action you could take? What if someone was being bullied on the playground, and you were nearby? Would you go for help? Like Jesus in the temple, if you saw something wrong, could you dare to do something? It might not be easy. It takes courage to stand up to our friends. Sometimes friendship with Jesus means daring to do something, even if it makes some people angry with us.

CONVERSATION STARTERS

What keeps you from standing up when you see something wrong?

What does it mean to be a good friend?

How do you think the other people who were in the Temple felt when Jesus flipped over the tables? Why?

WHERE TO FIND OUT MORE

Selling Cattle and Sheep: John 2:13–22

Overturning Tables: Mark 11:15–19

Driving Out Salesmen: Matthew 21:12–13 and Luke 19:45–46

A PRAYER

Jesus, thank you for promising to be with me in every situation, especially when I am standing up for what is right. You said that all things are possible with God. Please give me the courage to stand up for what is right, even when it is difficult to do so. Amen.

One of the Toughest Things about Friendship

It is difficult to keep forgiving when people continue doing wrong to us. Peter once asked Jesus how many times we need to forgive someone. The questioner thought seven times was a lot. Jesus gave a surprising answer. He said we have to forgive "seventy times seven" times, which really meant that we should have no limit on our forgiveness. He explained by using a story about why we must forgive again, and again, and again.

A king found out that a servant owed him a great deal of money, so he decided to collect. But the man had no way to pay it back. The king planned to take all the man's property and put the man and his whole family in jail. The servant fell to his knees and begged the king to be patient. He promised to pay back everything. Moved with compassion, the king let the servant go and even forgave the loan. The man was free of debt!

This is how God forgives us.

But the man in Jesus' story made a bad choice. He went to a fellow servant who owed him a much smaller amount than what he had owed the king. The man grabbed his fellow servant, started to choke him, and demanded his money back! When this fellow fell on his knees and begged for mercy, the man refused it. He had that servant thrown in jail. When people saw this, they grew upset that the man forgiven so much refused to forgive someone else. They told the king, who called the man in and said, *"You wicked servant! I forgave you your entire debt because you begged me to. Should you not have had pity on your fellow servant, as I had pity on you?" Then in anger [the king] handed him over to the torturers until he should pay back the whole debt* (Matthew 18:32–34).

Jesus warned that we must forgive if we want to be forgiven. Every person does things that offend God, who willingly forgives everyone. But, to fully embrace God's forgiveness, we must also forgive others.

It's really important for us to help one another forgive those who hurt us. Jesus said that if someone sins against you, you should go to them in private and discuss it. If they listen, you have renewed the friendship. But if they don't listen, Jesus suggests bringing another person into the conversation to help the one who harmed you to see the mistake. Hopefully having another person with you will change the person's mind, and correct the fault. The goal is to heal broken relationships. Jesus promises to help you grow your friendships, even when it's not easy.

CONVERSATION STARTERS

According to Jesus' parable, how are we to treat others when it comes to forgiveness?

What part of the Lord's Prayer (the Our Father) reminds us about forgiveness?

Who can you turn to when you need help with forgiveness?

WHERE TO FIND OUT MORE

Turn the Other Cheek: Matthew 5:39–47

Forgive Repeatedly: Matthew 18:15–20, 21–35

The Golden Rule: Matthew 7:12

◇◇◇◇◇◇◇◇◇◇◇◇◇◇◇◇◇◇◇◇

A PRAYER

Jesus, you are full of mercy, and you know how I feel. You see everything. You even see the things that aren't fair that happen to me and to people I love. The world is not always fair. Jesus, you ask me to love and forgive anyway. Sometimes this feels impossible, but I know that you can help me do the impossible. Help me, Jesus. Thank you for your good example. I put my trust in you. Amen.

◇◇◇◇◇◇◇◇◇◇◇◇◇◇◇◇◇◇◇◇◇◇◇◇◇

[Jesus asked,]

"Do you love me?"

—*John 21:17*

Peter Dives In

What do you do when a friendship is broken? You might be tempted to stay angry, stop talking to someone, or withhold forgiveness. But Jesus shows us another way. He gave us some great examples of what to do when a friendship suffers. One example is Jesus' friendship with Peter, who really wanted to stay friends with Jesus forever. How did Peter damage their friendship to begin with?

When Jesus was arrested, Peter wanted to see what was happening, but he was afraid of getting arrested too. So Peter followed the crowd and watched from a short distance. Three times people asked Peter if he knew Jesus, and each time, Peter said no. Later, Peter realized he had betrayed Jesus by pretending that he didn't know him. Peter was overwhelmed by his failure, and he ran off and cried bitterly. How could he ever ask Jesus to forgive him?

After Jesus rose from the dead, he appeared to all the Apostles in a room where they were hiding for fear of being arrested and killed. Jesus wished them all a lasting peace.

Perhaps Jesus could see that Peter needed something more. Jesus thought of a way to help Peter see that their broken friendship didn't stop Jesus from loving him, and so Jesus appeared to him again on another occasion.

Peter and some others were sitting around, not sure what to do next. Peter decided to go fishing, and several people followed. Even though the others knew that Peter was not perfect, they also knew how close he had been to Jesus.

A man on the beach watched as the group caught nothing. He yelled that they should try to throw their nets on the right side of the boat. There, he assured them, they would find something. They did, and the net nearly broke from the weight of so many fish. In that moment, John recognized that the man was Jesus.

When Peter heard this, he jumped out of the boat and swam to shore, eager to be with Jesus. When he got there, Jesus was calmly cooking fish over a fire. Jesus also had bread to share. Jesus started a conversation with Peter to show that all was forgiven.

Jesus never holds a grudge or seeks revenge, and he is always ready to forgive. True friendship means that we don't keep a record of wrongs. At the same time, Jesus wants us to express sorrow and mean it.

Jesus asked Peter three times, *"Do you love me?"* (John 21:17). Each time, Peter answered that he did. Jesus then asked him to take care of his sheep, which meant that Peter should lead the Church. After this, Peter knew that their friendship would last for Peter's entire life. Jesus warned Peter that several bad things would happen, but not to worry. Jesus would always be with him even when Peter couldn't see him anymore. *"Do not let your hearts be troubled [or afraid]"* (John 14:1). Jesus would remain through the invisible power of the Holy Spirit.

CONVERSATION STARTERS

Why do people have trouble saying they are sorry?

How might Jesus help us be more forgiving?

How is this miraculous catch of fish similar to the story told when Jesus first called Andrew, Peter, James, and John to follow him? (See Luke 5:1–11.)

WHERE TO FIND OUT MORE

Breakfast on the Beach: John 21:1–19

◇◇◇◇◇◇◇◇◇◇◇◇◇◇◇◇◇◇◇◇◇◇

A PRAYER

Think for a moment about someone you are angry with.
Maybe it's a friend who broke a promise and let you down.
Imagine that person standing in front of Jesus on the cross. Then imagine you are standing next to that person. Jesus forgave his killers and prayed out loud, "Father, forgive them. . ." (Luke 23:34). Take a few minutes of silence.
When you are ready, pray these words:

Forgiving Jesus, when I get angry, sometimes I am hurting inside.
Sometimes I feel too proud to forgive someone. Help me let go of what hurts.
Help me to be more like you: kind and forgiving.
I want to forgive as you did. You know how hard this is to do.
And please help me apologize when I should. Amen.

◇◇◇◇◇◇◇◇◇◇◇◇◇◇◇◇◇◇◇◇◇◇◇

[God's ways are] more precious to me

than heaps of silver and gold.

—*Psalm 119:72*

Friendship Is More Valuable than Money

Once, a rich man asked Jesus what he needed to do to reach his ultimate goal of friendship with Jesus: getting to heaven. Jesus reminded him to follow the commandments, which Jesus summed up as loving God and loving people. The man replied that he already did that. Jesus looked at him with love; he probably could see that this man really wanted to be close to God. Then he invited that man to sell everything and join Jesus and his group of close friends. The rich man went away sad because he had lots of stuff he didn't want to sell.

Jesus' friends were stunned when he said that it would be hard for rich people to enter heaven. And yet, we know that Jesus meant what he said because Jesus repeated this message at other times.

For example, he told a huge crowd that had gathered to hear him speak, *"Blessed are you who are poor, for the kingdom of God is yours"* (Luke 6:20).

This was said in Jesus' famous sermon on a mountain. Jesus went on to promise that poor people would own the kingdom of God. Jesus boldly announced that the first will be last *(Matthew 20:16)*. Jesus said some daring things. No wonder some people didn't like him.

Clothes, money, power, popularity? None of these things last like friendship with Jesus does, nor can they make people truly happy. Material possessions, fame, and wealth might make you feel good for a while. Eventually, though, you want something more meaningful. It's as if every person has a God-shaped hole that can never be filled with anything but God. But people *try* to get rid of that empty feeling by using *things* to fill the space that God created inside, the space that is designed only for friendship between God and humanity. Trying to fill that space with other things never works.

Jesus encouraged his friends not to be troubled when difficult things happen. He said that people who wept and mourned would be blessed, because some day they would be laughing joyfully when God's kingdom reigns on earth as it does in heaven.

Jesus didn't change his messages despite how people reacted. He said, *"Blessed are you who are now hungry, for you will be satisfied"* (Luke 6:21). He wanted his friends to focus on how wonderful God's kingdom is. With God, we lack nothing.

CONVERSATION STARTERS

Describe a time when you wanted something very badly, but when you got it, you were disappointed, or it didn't last, or you found yourself wanting something else.

When have you felt happy without buying anything?

In Jesus' sermon *(Matthew 5:44)*, he said we should love our enemies and pray for people who do us harm. Why would this make you happier than if you stayed angry or tried to get revenge?

WHERE TO FIND OUT MORE

Sermon on the Mount: Matthew 5:1—7:29

Sermon on the Plain: Luke 6:20–49

Be Light: Matthew 5:14–16

What Is Heaven Like? Matthew 20:1–16

Rich Man Leaves Sad: Matthew 19:16–30

◇◇◇◇◇◇◇◇◇◇◇◇◇◇◇◇◇◇◇◇◇◇◇

A PRAYER

*Dear Jesus, you said that we would be blessed by being peacemakers
and merciful, and that God will show us mercy.
You also said that if we mourn, you will comfort us.
You want me to recognize that no matter what, you are with me.
Remove any roadblocks
that keep me from a closer friendship with you. Amen.*

◇◇◇◇◇◇◇◇◇◇◇◇◇◇◇◇◇◇◇◇◇◇◇

The disciples approached Jesus and said,

"Who is the greatest in the kingdom of heaven?"

[Jesus] called a child over.

—*Matthew 18:1–2*

Who Has the Greatest Friendship?

One day, the disciples asked Jesus who is greatest in God's Kingdom. They wondered whose friendship was the best, and if they might be seen as the greatest since they were following Jesus.

Jesus surprised them by calling a child forward. He said, *"Unless you turn and become like children, you will not enter the kingdom of heaven"* (Matthew 18:3).

Jesus said, *"Whoever humbles himself like this child is the greatest in the kingdom of heaven"* (Matthew 18:4). Jesus considers true friendship to involve humbly depending on God.

Jesus understood that kids don't have much power. They must ask permission from parents, teachers, and other adults to do almost everything. They usually don't have much money, they can't drive, they can't choose their own bedtimes, and they can't eat whatever they want. Children are *dependent*.

In Psalm 1 we hear that we should be like trees that need the soil around their roots. Without nutrients and water that trees get through soil, the trees would be dead. Trees can't get up and walk to a place where water is. In a very real way, trees are humble and dependent.

Jesus wants *us* to be like trees growing near running water, and having strong roots as a result. And a short tree is not better than a tall one, nor a tall tree better than a short one. We all matter.

We will grow strong and experience greatness by depending upon friendship with Jesus—*if* our roots go deep into the "soil" of God's love.

CONVERSATION STARTERS

How would you feel if you were that child Jesus called over to stand in the middle of the group?

Who do you depend upon?

Describe someone who is humble. Do you know anyone who is humble? What are some of the things you like about this person?

WHERE TO FIND OUT MORE

Prayers for Many Occasions: the Book of Psalms

Become Like Children: Matthew 18:1–5; 10

◇◇◇◇◇◇◇◇◇◇◇◇◇◇◇◇◇◇

A PRAYER

Take a few quiet moments. Imagine yourself and other children sitting in front of Jesus who is speaking kindly and gently to the group. What does he say? How does it make you feel? Then slowly read Psalm 23, pausing often. Ask Jesus any question that comes to mind, and listen. Close by saying Thank you and Amen.

◇◇◇◇◇◇◇◇◇◇◇◇◇◇◇◇◇◇

[Jesus said,] "Ask and it will be given to you;

seek and you will find;

knock and the door will be opened to you."

—*Matthew 7:7*

Friendship Allows Us to Talk Directly to God

Good friendships involve conversations. Did you know that one way to pray is to simply talk to Jesus as if you could see him sitting or standing right next to you?

One of Jesus' friends asked what was the best way to pray. Jesus said that, when we pray, we should address God as "Abba" which means "papa" or "daddy." Jesus wants us to know that God our Father is easy to talk to. Then he shared with his friends an important prayer. In Hebrew, this prayer rhymes, which made it easier for everyone to remember it in the days before books were common. This prayer does not rhyme in English. You will recognize it right away:

Our Father in heaven,
hallowed be your name,
your kingdom come,
your will be done,
on earth as in heaven.
Give us today our daily bread;
and forgive us our debts,
as we forgive our debtors;
and do not subject us to the final test,
but deliver us from the evil one.

(Matthew 6:9–13)

Good Question!

What are debtors and trespassers?

Matthew's Gospel uses the word "debts" to refer to our sins. We "owe" it to God to be truly sorry for our sins. Therefore, Jesus asks us to forgive anyone who does harm and sins against us. In a way, sin is like ignoring a NO TRESPASSING sign. We ask God to forgive the times we've trespassed against God's laws by failing to love, which is a sin.

In this prayer, called the Our Father, Jesus emphasizes that we are to forgive others in the same way that God our Father forgives us. Friendship with God demands forgiveness.

And Jesus knew that God always hears our prayer. Like a good friend, God might be listening without saying anything. It feels really good to be heard, doesn't it? You can have conversations with God the Father and Jesus, but it's not always easy to hear what God communicates back.

This is one reason silence is an important part of prayer. We should not be doing all the talking! In moments of silence, God might pop a loving idea into your head. God also "talks" through feelings of peace, love, joy, and hope. In true friendship we care about emotions. If you pay attention to how you feel, you will hear God's messages more clearly.

CONVERSATION STARTERS

How do you imagine Jesus would talk to God?

Who taught you the Our Father? Is there a line in this prayer that you like best?

Is there something in the Our Father that you don't understand?

WHERE TO FIND OUT MORE

Pray Like This: Matthew 6:1–21

Forgive: Mark 11:25–26

How to Pray: Luke 11:1–13

◇◇◇◇◇◇◇◇◇◇◇◇◇◇◇◇◇◇◇◇◇

A PRAYER

Thoughtful Jesus, thank you for teaching us the Our Father.
You invite me to talk to God as I would talk to a loving parent.
You told us that you are one with the Father. You made everything good,
Jesus, and you always listen to me. Every day you give me what I need
so that I can be a loving person. Jesus, you forgave. You demonstrated mercy.
Help me to forgive even when it's hard. Amen.

◇◇◇◇◇◇◇◇◇◇◇◇◇◇◇◇◇◇◇◇◇

When he was insulted, he returned no insult;

when he suffered, he did not threaten;

instead, he handed himself over

to the one who judges justly.

—*1 Peter 2:23*

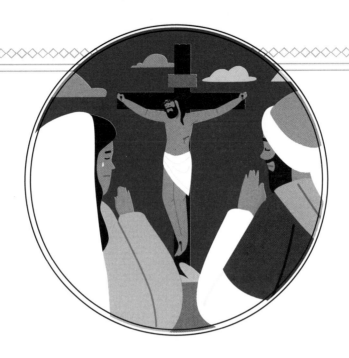

Suffering and Friendship

Friends are willing to share one another's worries and concerns, what the Bible calls burdens. Jesus took on every burden for every person for all time when he allowed himself to be arrested and hung on a cross. Before he died, he spent the night in a prison cell. Maybe he couldn't sleep. Certainly, he was hurting. The soldiers had beaten him badly with a whip and had hit him many times. They had pushed a crown of thorns into his scalp. This physical abuse weakened Jesus' body. He must have been in great pain.

Jesus suffered greatly, and because of this we are able to unite our suffering with his because Jesus understands what it's like to suffer.

Jesus' suffering teaches us many things. What can we learn from Jesus' suffering?

From Jesus' example, we can discover what to do during hard times: *allow friends to help.* When Jesus had to carry his cross, his human body could hardly lift it. Guards pulled from the crowd of onlookers a man from Cyrene named Simon to help Jesus carry his cross. Sometimes people feel too proud to let themselves receive support from others. That's not the model Jesus provides.

We can also come to understand that *every person alive will have to go through difficult times,* and when we do, *Jesus will be there for us,* often through friends and family. Jesus did not suffer alone, and we are not meant to either. God provides family and friends to support us. Refusing help can be a sin of pride. It's like saying, "I don't need you, or anyone else. I am in control—not God."

When we suffer, *we grow in compassion.* Because of our own suffering, we are better at understanding other people when they suffer. Paul wrote to people in Galatia, *"Bear one another's burdens"* (Galatians 6:2). Of course, we do not help others so we can demand pay-back, make them feel that they owe us something, or give in to the temptation to judge that we're better than someone else.

Paul also wrote, *"Bear your share of hardship for the gospel with the strength that comes from God"* (2 Timothy 1:8). Jesus did that. We see from Jesus' example that God gives us courage and strength during difficulties.

Suffering doesn't make sense when we're going through it, but later it might. In some cases, we will never know why suffering happens, but surely God can do good work in our lives, even through our suffering.

Be on the lookout for ways you see people helping each other. Accepting someone's help can be a way of following Jesus, and a doorway to a new friendship.

CONVERSATION STARTERS

Who has helped you in challenging times?

Who have you helped, and how?

What does community mean to you? How do you help your church community to be stronger and friendlier?

WHERE TO FIND OUT MORE

Take Up Your Cross Daily: Matthew 16:24, Mark 8:34, and Luke 9:23

Simon the Cyrene: Matthew 27:32, Mark 15:21, and Luke 23:26

Faithful Friends: Sirach 6:14–17

◇◇◇◇◇◇◇◇◇◇◇◇◇◇◇◇◇◇◇◇◇◇

A PRAYER

Faithful Jesus, thank you for showing us that we should let others help. Thank you for people who offer me a hand. Open my heart to know when I should accept help, and when I should give it. Amen.

◇◇◇◇◇◇◇◇◇◇◇◇◇◇◇◇◇◇◇◇◇◇

[Jesus said,] "And behold,

I am with you always."

—*Matthew 28:20*

PART 4:
JESUS LIVES!

For the sake of the joy that lay before him

he endured the cross.

—*Hebrews 12:2*

An Eternal Kingdom

At a parade, people strain to see what's coming down the road. They cheer and wave flags, sparklers, or pom poms. It's exciting.

When, after three years of publicly speaking about God's love, Jesus came to Jerusalem, which was the holiest city of that time, people threw a welcoming parade in his honor. They tore palm branches from trees to wave as he passed by and used them to carpet the ground as Jesus rode a donkey into the city.

But some people wondered. A king on a donkey? They thought a king should be mounted upon a beautiful horse, accompanied by legions of soldiers. What kind of king was Jesus? All he did was talk about love, kindness, forgiveness, sharing, and other ideas like those. They thought kings needed to be wealthy, superior, bossy, and proud.

The secret was out: Jesus would be a different kind of king.

And Jesus is a unique ruler. He lives forever! His kingdom extends between heaven and earth.

Jesus taught and showed us what it means to live as members of God's Kingdom. One powerful lesson occurred at the Last Supper where Jesus surprised everyone by doing what slaves did in those days. He knelt in front of the Apostles. One by one he washed their feet, which got dirty quickly because they wore sandals and all the roads were unpaved. When Jesus came to Peter, Peter didn't want Jesus to wash his feet. Was he too proud to let Jesus serve him? Jesus told Peter that humble service was part of friendship with him and his heavenly Father.

Good Question!

What happened at the Last Supper?

Jesus planned and provided the best meal ever. He turned ordinary bread into his real body. While people all over the city were celebrating the Jewish holiday called Passover, which involved eating lamb sacrificed at their temple, Jesus ate a final formal meal before being arrested and crucified. The Last Supper demonstrated that Jesus now was God's Lamb. At Mass we always say, "Lamb of God. . ." before people receive Holy Communion. Jesus lives forever in the Eucharist.

Jesus set an example he wants us to imitate: being a leader is the opposite of having a position of pride and power. It means we should be humble. We should take every opportunity to serve others.

As Catholics, we believe Jesus is alive, resurrected, and present physically with us in the Eucharist. When we receive Holy Communion, we take Jesus into our bodies. Jesus lives! We remember the past when Jesus walked among his people, and we celebrate that Jesus is with us *now*. Someday, we will be together in heaven, the eternal kingdom, which lasts forever. That is *really* good news.

Jesus gave us the gift of the Eucharist during his last supper on earth. He eagerly wished to establish a new kind of meal with his dearest friends and family, built on their past traditions. He wanted them to always remember his actions, and to repeat them with their children, who would pass them on to their children, and eventually to us.

Jesus longed to say many things to his friends before he died. The next time they would eat together would be after he rose from the dead. Imagine what his mother Mary thought as she listened to her son speak at this final supper. She probably never suspected that one of his Apostles, Judas, was planning to turn Jesus over to the authorities, just for money, that very night! But knowing Jesus better than anyone, she understood that life involves sorrows. After Jesus rose from the dead, Mary would join the early Christian community to remember Jesus' final meal and recognize that *Jesus still lives*. The Eucharist that Jesus gave us at the Last Supper is what we share every time we go to Mass.

CONVERSATION STARTERS

When you go to Mass, what part usually catches your attention?

Have you ever been to Mass in another city or country? If so, what was different? What was the same?

If you could speak to Jesus right now, what question would you ask him?

WHERE TO FIND OUT MORE

Jesus Is God and Human: John 8:58 and Exodus 3:14–15. (Jesus says, *"Before Abraham came to be, I AM."* When Moses asked God for his name, God said, *"I am who I am."*)

Jesus Said, "I Am the Bread of Life": John 6:35

Jesus Is the Way, the Truth, and Life: John 14:6

<><><><><><><><><><><><><>

A PRAYER

Jesus, you lived an ordinary life, but you were extraordinary.
Sometimes people could see that, and sometimes they couldn't.
Forgive me when I don't pay attention to you, and when I skip praying.
Please give me the help I need to love always. Thank you. Amen.

<><><><><><><><><><><><><>

Friends Tell: He's Alive!

People love to share good news. Imagine your dad telling you to let your brother know that the family is going on vacation to your favorite amusement park. You would probably hurry to tell your brother this great news.

That must be how Mary Magdalene felt when she encountered Jesus after he rose from the dead, and he asked her to tell his friends that *he lives*! She was the first person to see him alive again. And she was the first person to announce the resurrection of Jesus to others.

Early in Jesus' ministry, he had healed Mary Magdalene. Then she provided financial support to Jesus as he and his disciples traveled and made friends. Mary Magdalene stood with Jesus' mother as Jesus died, and also when Jesus was taken down from the cross. She followed the men who buried Jesus so that she could see the grave and remember where it was. As a close friend, Mary bravely went to his grave on the third day after he died.

It was just around sunrise.

The grave was being guarded because the people responsible for executing Jesus did not want to take any chances. They knew that Jesus had spoken about coming back to life. What if Jesus' friends and followers stole his body from the grave and then claimed he had risen from the dead? That would cause all kinds of trouble for people in power. So the Roman officials ordered strong soldiers to guard the entrance to Jesus' tomb around the clock.

But on the third day, the earth shook, and rocks tumbled.

The tomb was empty. Jesus had risen!

Mary Magdalene hurried to tell Peter who, along with another disciple, ran to the tomb and found it empty, as Mary had described.

Later, Mary was standing outside of the empty tomb crying. Jesus told her to go to his followers and tell them the good news that *he lives.* She ran to them and said, *"I have seen the Lord"* (John 20:18).

This is how Mary Magdalene, who was a very close friend of Jesus, became known as the Apostle to the Apostles.

CONVERSATION STARTERS

Who was your best friend growing up? Who is your best friend now? Why?

What's the best news you ever heard? How have you shared it?

How do you think your life would change if you made Jesus your best friend?

WHERE TO FIND OUT MORE

Mary Meets Jesus: John 20:11–18

◇◇◇◇◇◇◇◇◇◇◇◇◇◇◇◇◇◇◇

A PRAYER

Imagine the day of Jesus' resurrection, and you visit Jesus' tomb.
You peek into the grave because the stone is no longer blocking the entrance.
It's cold and damp in the cave. You don't want to stay there!
You hear Jesus call your name. You turn toward his voice.
You are staring into a very bright light.
Look right into his face. How does Jesus look at you?
Give thanks that Jesus lives! Thank Jesus for being with you right now.
Finish with Amen.

◇◇◇◇◇◇◇◇◇◇◇◇◇◇◇◇◇◇◇

[Jesus said,] "Do not be afraid any longer,

little flock, for your Father is pleased

to give you the kingdom."

—*Luke 12:32*

God with Us Today

Knowing Jesus as a friend means that he is with you here and now. He's not some dead person from long ago. Jesus lives now, even if you can't physically see him with your eyes. The Bible tells us that Jesus is the image of the invisible God.

When you close your eyes, you can't see the room you are in, but the room is still there. A name that we use for Jesus during Advent, Emmanuel, means "God with us." Jesus will never leave us alone, even if we feel alone.

And Jesus is with us in the Eucharist that we receive at Mass.

At Mass, you will see the priest pour water into the chalice that holds a little wine. Once the water combines with the wine, no one can tell which part is which. They *cannot* be separated. Just as the water and wine mix and become one, so are we one with Jesus.

◇◇

Good Question!

What is a Chalice?

A chalice is an ancient style of cup on a stem used at Mass to hold the wine that will become the precious blood of the risen Christ. It might be made of gold or silver, or it may be a work of ceramic art. Whatever it's made of, this is no ordinary cup.

The water didn't stop being water when it went into the wine, nor did the wine stop being wine. And yet, two substances completely and irreversibly become one.

The same is true of Jesus, who is a human person exactly like us, except he never sinned, and at the same time, Jesus is God, who created everything.

When we pray the Creed, we use a big word: *consubstantial.* It means that Jesus is the same *substance* as God and at the same time he is the same *substance* as you and me. He is both. You cannot separate God from the human person Jesus.

This mystery is impossible to understand. We can't even imagine how amazing God is. God made everything, including things that are normally not visible. For example, the Church is one family. Wherever Catholics are in the world, they use the same Scripture readings at Mass but in different languages. We become visible as one family of God.

The body of Christ also becomes visible. It happens when people receive Jesus in Holy Communion. Catholics believe that Jesus is truly present—body, blood, soul, and divinity—under the appearance of bread and wine. When the priest or Eucharistic minister holds up the host and says, "the body of Christ," we respond, "Amen!" which means, "I really believe that is true."

People today continue to encounter Jesus whenever they love others and when they allow other people to love them. Jesus is present wherever and whenever people truly love each other. So be sure to listen when people tell you their true stories of knowing Jesus.

Jesus lives.

CONVERSATION STARTERS

To praise is to acknowledge someone's greatness. How might you praise Jesus right now?

Do you find it easy to talk to Jesus? Why or why not?

Why do you think that Jesus never stops reaching out to make new friends?

WHERE TO FIND OUT MORE

Don't Be Troubled: John 14:1

Holy Spirit, Our Helper: John 14:26

You Will Receive Power: Acts 1:8

At Mass: Listen for the priest quietly praying these words as he pours a few drops of water into the wine: "By the mystery of this water in wine, may we come to share in the divinity of Christ, who humbled himself to share in our humanity."

A PRAYER

Hi, Jesus! I know you want us to be best friends. I feel safe and confident confiding in you and telling you about my day. I can come to you when I need help. That's what friends do. I trust you to be my friend no matter what happens in life. Thank you! Amen.

Beloved, let us love one another,

because love is of God; everyone who loves

is begotten by God and knows God.

—1 John 4:7

Epilogue: Jesus and the Mystery That Is God

Imagine that you are a small cup at the beach, and you are full of ocean water. You cannot hold much water, and certainly the whole ocean cannot fit inside you. You would know things like the ocean's color and temperature, but you would not know where the ocean touches China or where it is deepest; you would not know about all the fascinating creatures that live underwater.

If God were that ocean, and you were bobbing along as a small plastic cup, you would be held and surrounded by God. But you could never know everything there is to know about this enormous ocean that is God. You could love being in the "ocean" even though you don't understand much about it.

Many people have tried to figure out how one God can also be a Trinity of Father, Jesus the Son, and Holy Spirit. One such person was Augustine of Hippo, a saint who lived about 400 years after Jesus. There is a story about Augustine feeling frustrated by not being able to understand God. One day, while walking along a seashore, Augustine noticed a boy running back and forth with a bucket, each time pouring water into a shallow hole, where the water quickly disappeared. Augustine asked the boy what he was doing. "I'm trying to put the sea in this hole," the boy replied. Augustine told the boy he would never fit the sea in the tiny hole. The boy looked up with a smile. He replied that neither could Augustine fit everything there is to know about God into his brain. Augustine realized that God was using the boy to deliver a message: God is a mystery we cannot fully understand.

Even so, we *can* know certain things about the Holy Trinity. For example, we know that Jesus described God as a family. God is father, and Jesus is the son. The Holy Spirit is God's invisible, loving presence that is everywhere. Their love for one another is so great and intimate, they are One. We are invited to live our lives within these loving relationships.

Our heavenly Father loves us beyond measure. That's why God sent Jesus to give us an example of how to live. And the Holy Spirit lives in us to remind us that God always desires to shower us with gifts of love, joy, peace, patience, gentleness, and more.

We long to meet God face-to-face and experience joy beyond our wildest dreams in heaven. Jesus promised that in heaven, we will have eternal life. But, like small plastic cups filled with ocean water, we cannot know everything about heaven and eternal life now. What's more important is to know that we are made in God's image, that we are made to be good, and that God loves us far beyond our ability to ever understand. Always.

ACKNOWLEDGMENTS

Being a grandmother to 11 people made writing this book a gift to them and to myself. While I was writing, we read stories aloud and then discussed them. My grandchildren helped me with their *good questions*. I hope you have as many great conversations as we did. We opened windows into our souls: privileged places. Thank you to editorial consultants Ted, Leo, and David Pehanich; Helena Pierce; and Kirra, Mikayla, and Julisa Provence. To Cecilia Pehanich, and Preston and Olivia Pierce: I hope you will enjoy reading this book when you get older. To future generations of our families: same!

And special thanks to my long-suffering and beloved husband Steve Pehanich, who supported me in countless ways. Gratitude goes to our four children, too: Sarah, Tony, Liliana, and John. I'm grateful to other readers: A great teacher, reading specialist, and mom, Laurel Pehanich; a fabulous grandma Connie Koppes and her daughter-in-law Amanda; a talented writer and mother, Kristy Tucker; and some anonymous angels.

Thank you, Maura Poston, for your devotion while editing this book. And thank you, Gary Jansen, for inviting me to write it.

I'm grateful for my friends and family in heaven, including Mother Mary, her Son Jesus, and the entirety of the holy family of God whose example and prayers encouraged me. See you at the big party in heaven!

ABOUT THE AUTHOR

Loretta Pehanich has served the Church in myriad ways, from catechist, lector, and Eucharistic Minister to small group leader, Bible study facilitator, diocesan employee, writer for a number of nonprofits, parish capital campaign consultant, retreat speaker, and more. An Ignatian-trained spiritual director, Loretta has been accompanying people in their walks with God since 2012.

Loretta is a freelance writer and the author of, among other books, *A Book of Grace-Filled Days 2022* (Loyola Press) and *Women In Conversation* (RENEW International). Loretta's monthly blogs can be found at www.IgnatianSpirituality.com.